THE GLUE

MIKE STEVENS

Printed 2017

www.mikebstevens.com
mike@mikebstevens.com

National Library of Australia Cataloguing-in-Publication entry:

Creator:	Stevens, Mike, author.
Title:	The glue : relationship as the connection for effective youth ministry / Mike Stevens.
ISBN:	9781640082151 (paperback)
Subjects:	Church work with youth. Christian leadership.

Design and Layout: Les Colston - les@urbanzeal.com.au

CONTENTS

ACKNOWLEDGEMENTS   9

FOREWORD   11

INTRODUCTION   15

SECTION ONE **BIG ROCKS GO FIRST**   21
  SECTION ONE REFLECTIONS   42

SECTION TWO **LEADING YOURSELF**   47
  SECTION TWO REFLECTIONS   66

SECTION THREE **LEADING OTHERS**   71
  SECTION THREE REFLECTIONS   126

SECTION FOUR **YOUTH MINISTRY ESSENTIALS**   131
  SECTION FOUR REFLECTIONS   179

SECTION FIVE **FUTURE FOCUS**   185
  SECTION FIVE REFLECTIONS   208

SECTION SIX **FINAL THOUGHTS**   213

APPENDIX 1   220

APPENDIX 2   222

BIBLIOGRAPHY   223

For Ella, Ben and Lucy

You are the next generation and I love you.

Psalm 71: 18-19

ACKNOWLEDGEMENTS

I want to thank the people who have generously invested into my life over the years. From leaders taking a risk on me, to youth being willing to follow some of my crazy ideas for the gospel. In particular, I thank the Charge young people and leaders at Golden Grove Baptist and the Surge young people and leaders at Crossway Baptist. I loved being your Youth Pastor and serving you.

I would like to thank the following leaders who have shaped my life and relational approach to leadership. Thanks to Mark Wilkinson, Scott Hawkins, Scott Berry, Jason Lippitt, Rod Denton, Russell Eley, Jason Hoet, Dale Stephenson, Carey Nieuwhof, Margaret Spicer, Julian Dunham, Mike Mills, and my parents, Trevor and Helen Stevens, who modelled to me from an early age the importance of loving God and loving people.

A massive thanks to the people who have helped make this book happen. Les Colston at Urban Zeal, Rachel Davison and Wendy Noble for editing, Gavin Brown for writing a reflection at the end of each section and giving me honest feedback on the book contents, and the Baptist Churches of SA for sponsoring the release.

To Michelle and my three beautiful children – thanks for being patient with me. As this project gathered momentum you have shown me grace and released me to give it the attention it needed. I love you and am so grateful we get to do life together.

FOREWORD

The significance of relationship in the disciple making process of a young person cannot be overstated. Sometimes we have to ask questions of those who have left the church to understand how we should conduct ourselves with those who have stayed. On two separate occasions, I have been involved with exit interviews for churches. The question has been simple, "Why did you leave this church?" We found out there were many different answers as to why a person would leave a church. Outside of some sort of catastrophic failure which would give a common reply most people leave the church for a plethora of reasons.

It was almost by accident that we stumbled onto a single reason as to why people left. Somebody asked whether Sunday was the exclusive point of contact that the person had with the church. With a positive response to this question more people were asked the same question. We discovered a staggering 93% of people who had left the church had this one thing in common: Sunday was their exclusive point of contact with the church. This caused me to develop the metaphor of the travellator from the front door to the back door of the church.

We have all seen a travellator, it is like a moving footpath at the airport. When you stand still you are still moving because the travellator is moving you. So, the idea that there is a travellator from the front door to the back door of any church means that a person simply has to stand still and they are moving towards the back door, choosing to leave the church. This is true even for those who have just arrived. If the worship service is their exclusive point of contact with the church, they are choosing to leave, even if they have only just arrived. The travellator is taking them towards the back door. This same principle is true for young people. In the absence of relationship young people are choosing to leave the very environment that I should be helping them to become a disciple of Jesus.

What people need to do is to step into community. This is because relationship is the glue. In the absence of relationship people have a small voice inside them that says "This is not enough." It is telling them the truth but it tends to be applied incorrectly. Most people, when they hear this voice, choose to change churches or choose to leave altogether. What they should've done is to step into community as this is where relationship happens and relationship is essential to discipleship.

I worked together with Pastor Mike Stevens for 4 years at Crossway Baptist Church in Melbourne, Australia. We have remained friends since he moved on. When you meet Mike Stevens in person with his bright eyes, he is so engaged. When you talk to him you have his undivided attention. His disarming gaze is but a foretaste of his whole ministry philosophy: Relationship is the glue.

Mike is a practitioner. He has a passion in his heart to see all people become disciples of Jesus. With years of experience in Youth Ministry this book is part of his legacy, his contribution back into Youth Ministry. The idea that "disciples are handmade not mass produced" has captivated Mike's heart and mind. He has established a relational grid to help young people become followers of Jesus.

This book is full of pithy insights causing the reader to reflect on some of the most important things about ministry to youth. If you are involved in ministry to young people you will be more than aware of the huge challenges that exist in helping a young person to follow Jesus. If you choose to take the time to read this book you will be exposing yourself to somebody who is invested many years of their life into ministering effectively to young people. You will discover, as Mike has, that, "Relationship is the glue." Read it, digest it, apply it and you will become a more effective discipler of young people.

Rev Dr Dale Stephenson
Senior Pastor, Crossway Baptist Church

INTRODUCTION

What is Relational Discipleship?

In "You Lost Me" lead researcher and best selling author David Kinnaman said, "Disciples are handmade not mass produced."[1] This phrase has stayed with me as I've wrestled with what it is to be an effective Youth Pastor and minister of the gospel. There is nothing closer to my heart than to see young people in the church and in the local community become handmade disciples of Jesus. This is a big but very worthy challenge.

This makes me think about what we do in youth ministry and consider just what is our main game. I'm convinced that at the very core of handmade disciples is a practice called relational discipleship. Young people desperately need significant adults willing to walk alongside them, to help them grow up in God's

---

[1] David Kinnaman, *You Lost Me: Why Young Christians Are Leaving Church and Rethinking Faith* (Grand Rapids, Michigan: Baker Books, 2011), 13.

ways. Church life and youth ministry isn't like a bread factory where infants grow into young people on some sort of conveyor belt and get neatly packaged ready for adulthood. Relational discipleship is the process of caring for and loving each young person in such a way that they feel free to grow in their faith by wrestling through questions and doubts in a safe and loving community.

In fact, relational discipleship is much like a beautiful handmade Moroccan rug. My wife and I travelled to Morocco and checked out the local produce. We spent time in the winding streets, taking in all the wonderful sights and smells. We also had the opportunity to visit where the Moroccan rugs were made. Each rug we saw was handmade. They were amazing! Although well out of our price range, we could see how much time, care and love went into making each one. They were made of the finest wool, hand-woven, like a piece of art. How much more precious then is each young person in our church and local community? It was Paul who said to the church in Ephesus, "For we are God's handiwork, created in Christ Jesus to do good works, which God prepared in advance for us to do."[2] The Greek word for handiwork in this verse is

2 Ephesians 2: 10

poiema which is where we get the words *poem* and *poetry*. It means we are God's poem, his poetry, his piece of art. We are special to God and He has a great plan for our lives, as we live for King Jesus.[3]

We have each been made by a loving God who has a redemptive plan for our lives. If we have found this new life through Jesus, we have the opportunity to walk alongside the next generation, helping them to understand that each individual is God's work of art and that He has a great plan for their lives. The way we can do this is through relationships. **Relationship is the glue** that enables us to have an intimate connection with Jesus and with the young people He has placed in our care.

The challenge before us is to take hold of this opportunity; taking time to shape our ministries around relational discipleship so that the youth in our care grow up with a faith that is robust and ready for adulthood. No mass produced model can make this happen. It takes a careful handmade approach engaged in the life of each individual.

[3] Tom Wright, *Paul for Everyone: The Prison Letters* (London, UK: SPCK, 2004), 24.

What This Book Is…

This book is a collection of many ideas, with the paradigm of relational discipleship at the core of each one. Each insight is intended to be read and digested by engaging with the final application questions. It is my hope that the contents of this book will encourage you in your own walk with Jesus, point you towards healthy leadership development pathways, and enable you to focus on the essential practices of effective ministry, whilst also wrestling with what the future landscape of youth ministry will look like.

Each section of this book draws from my own experiences, both personally and professionally, of over 12 years in paid youth ministry and close to 20 years of working with young people. My prayer is you will find challenge and hope and become a better person and leader from engaging with its contents. I have asked a wonderful Youth Pastor and my good friend, Gavin Brown, to write a reflection at the end of each section to assist you in hearing what God is saying and what you will do as a result.

My heart is to see well-formed handmade disciples for this generation and into the future, and I'm convinced God wants us to lean in and embrace this Kingdom challenge. I hope this book adds to this conversation and you are blessed as you read and engage with it.

Many blessings,

Mike Stevens

BIG ROCKS GO FIRST

Sean Covey in his worldwide best seller, *The 7 Habits of Highly Effective Teens,* talks about the big rock experiment.[4] If you have a bucket and need to fill it with rocks, pebbles and sand, the best strategy is to place the rocks first. Once the rocks, which are the biggest items, are in position you can then add the pebbles, followed by the sand. The sand will make its way through the cracks and gaps. Covey talks about this in terms of time management and using your diary. However, I think the same principle applies to ministry: effective youth ministers place the big rocks first, not only in their lives, but also in their ministry settings.

---

[4] Sean Covey, *The 7 Habits of Highly Effective Teens* (New York, USA: Fireside, 1998), 114.

This leaves me with a significant question to ask at the beginning of this book: what are the 'big rocks' of youth ministry? What should be prioritised and addressed first?

I've identified the following insights to explore in Section 1:

1: FOLLOW YOUR CALLING

2: PEOPLE > PROGRAMS

3: RELATIONAL CURRENCY

4: EVENT AND JOURNEY

5: DISCIPLE-MAKING PATHWAYS

6: MULTIPLY YOURSELF

BIG ROCK 1:
FOLLOW YOUR CALLING

A few years ago, I celebrated my thirtieth birthday with a sports themed party. It was a special night with friends from all different parts of my life. As happens at parties, we paused midway through the evening for speeches. During the speeches, some of my close friends had me perform physical challenges like push ups and pull ups. It *was* a sports themed party, after all!

I took the opportunity with a captive audience to give a little speech of my own and shared from my heart. I spoke about how God created us out of love to make a difference in this life for the sake of His Kingdom. I asked everyone to imagine what would happen if all of us chose to make a difference in our lives (as teachers, builders, students, plumbers, accountants, pastors, parents, husbands and wives, etc.) and then got back together in thirty years' time to tell the stories of all God had done amongst us. Wow! What a world we would be living in! I did have one cheeky fella say he wouldn't need to attend church the next day as he'd just heard the sermon.

This idea of making a difference in our world is something we all need to explore. With authenticity and integrity, we need to answer the question, 'What on earth am I here for?' or to put it another way, 'What is my calling?'

The best place to begin this conversation is by looking at the life and words of Jesus. If we smash together the Great Commandment[5] with the Great Commission[6] we get: **Love God with all you've got, love others as yourself, and go and make disciples of all nations.**

To take Jesus' words literally and seriously, we are on this earth to love God, love others and make disciples. This is our calling. This is the biggest rock of all that we need to believe and embody as pastors and leaders.

THIS IDEA OF MAKING A DIFFERENCE IN OUR WORLD IS SOMETHING WE ALL NEED TO EXPLORE.

[5] Matthew 22: 36-40

[6] Matthew 28: 18-20

How does your life reflect the core belief that we are on this earth to love God, love others and make disciples? How are you following the calling God has on your life?

BIG ROCK 2:

PEOPLE > PROGRAMS

It's often said that people are our biggest resource. It was Jim Collins who added to this by saying, "the *right* people are our biggest resource."[7] This is true. A person's good character will always trump competency, and having the right people around you and your team is essential. This affects how the team functions and how young people are cared for and discipled. In addition to people being our biggest resource, people are also our biggest opportunity, and the right people provide the biggest opportunities. Investing in people is core business for youth ministry, and maximising this lever of influence is key to maximising our effectiveness.

[7] Jim Collins, *Good to Great* (London, UK: Random House, 2001), 13.

Central to relational discipleship is the fundamental principle that people are more important than programs. Programs – the regular youth event, gathering a crowd around a common cause – is important, but this is not the end game. Regular youth programs are merely the vehicle for growing relationships with young people, so that trust can be developed and a formative discipleship journey can take place.

Close your eyes and remember when you were younger. (For some of us this can take a bit longer. Don't fall asleep when you close your eyes!) Think about high school, youth group, memorable sporting victories or music recitals. Now let your mind go to the people who invested in you: teachers, neighbours, coaches, bosses. What is it that stays with you? Why do they come to mind?

As I do this, my mind goes to a teacher called Mr Truman.[8] He was my Physical Education teacher: a good teacher and a great bloke who believed in me. He was honest about where I was skilled and where I needed to improve. He inspired me to study PE teaching at university. I also think of my first youth leader, Scott. He was a great leader who took time to get to know me and introduced

[8] Modbury High School, Adelaide, 1990s.

me to Jesus. He picked me up and dropped me home from youth group when I needed transport, and he always looked out for me.

My mind doesn't go to a specific school curriculum, a big youth event or even a camp; it goes to significant people who walked alongside and journeyed with me. However, without the structures of school and youth group, I would never have formed such deep and lasting relationships.

The program is important but people are more important. This is a big rock of youth ministry. The program is the vehicle that facilitates the formation of significant relationships.

Here are three initiatives that I've found particularly helpful in fostering a culture of people over programs.

1. Life Groups

Having regular life group nights in youth ministry works to elevate the value of people, creating a safe environment for people to go deeper in relationship. It also gives a specific focus for leaders, who follow up on six to eight young people and effectively become their Youth Pastor.

2. Hang Time

This creates space for spontaneous interaction and conversation between youth and leaders and youth and youth alike. This could take the form of intentional hang time at the beginning of youth group for 10–15 minutes, and another 30 minutes at the end of the night in a cafe style environment.

3. Relational Gatherings

A low-key games night or alternative, that requires a smaller amount of organisation and a higher level of relationship building, is really valuable in increasing the relational connection in your youth group.

What do you do in your context to foster a culture of people being more important than programs?

THE PROGRAM IS THE VEHICLE THAT FACILITATES THE FORMATION OF SIGNIFICANT RELATIONSHIPS.

RELATIONAL CURRENCY

Did you ever dream of being a rich Youth Pastor? Or ever think being in ministry would make you rich? I'm talking mega rich, like a billionaire. You can become a billionaire in youth ministry without becoming a criminal mastermind, you just need to use the right currency. If you want cash, ministry will probably never satisfy you. My advice would be to go and use your skills in communication and leadership, and start selling stuff. But if you want lasting impact in the lives of the young people and leaders you lead, then I have just the right currency for you. It's called relationship. Or as I like to call it, relational currency.

Every day we trade using relational currency. We make deposits and take withdrawals: from thanking a leader for going the extra mile (deposit); to encouraging a young person for bringing a friend to youth group (deposit); to asking leaders to step up for the clean-up (withdrawal), and to telling youth they can't leave the facility for a Slurpee at the local 7–11 (withdrawal). Every day, in the relationships we have, we are either making a deposit or taking a withdrawal, and sometimes both at the same time!

Relationship is the glue that holds our lives together, and it's the major catalyst in building trust and creating an environment to move towards shared Kingdom outcomes. Relational currency is valuable and needs to be traded with care. As I have mentioned, people are more important than programs and having healthy and loved people is the basis for a healthy and growing ministry. Whether you are meeting with a young person, a new leader or a parent, be intentional about depositing relational currency and love into their lives. There will inevitably be times when you need to make a withdrawal. It's our responsibility as leaders to make sure there is relational currency in the bank so the hard conversations can be had in a way that doesn't bankrupt the person involved.

When I study the life of Jesus I see a man who loved people. He invested relationally in the wellbeing of others. He made deposits and also took withdrawals from the people He was in relationship with. Consider his connection with Peter. He called Peter to be in relationship with Him and to become a fisher of people. He taught Peter how to love people, through word and deed, and gave him access to His life. He also spoke the hard word to Peter when he needed to hear it, and he restored Peter when he got it wrong. This was most obvious when Peter said he would never deny Jesus and Jesus said he would. Jesus took a relational withdrawal in that moment telling Peter what was going to happen, but what a deposit when Jesus restored him after He was resurrected.[9]

One simple way I affirm the value of people and become rich in relational currency, is the way I connect with people at church on a Sunday. This applies equally to a regular youth night. I love my church and I love the people God has brought into my life to serve and walk alongside. I love greeting people at the door, making eye contact and shaking as many hands as possible. I really enjoy spending time with people in the foyer, asking people how their week has been, and sitting with people after church when they are having a coffee or food just to say hi and check in. What I am doing is trying to follow the example of Jesus and make small deposits in the lives of people, building trust and growing relationships.

Think about your youth ministry now, your leadership team, your church; you are so rich! God has blessed you with each and every person in your midst. Why not say thanks to Him right now?

---

[9] The interactions of Jesus and Peter can be found at John 13: 31-38 (Jesus predicts Peter's denial), John 18 (Peter's denials) and John 21: 15-19 (Jesus reinstates Peter)

Relational Currency is a big rock of youth ministry. Where do you need to make a deposit? Where do you need to take a withdrawal?

EVENT AND JOURNEY

Youth Pastors love youth events: the fun games, the lights, the music, kids going nuts all over the property, a great message, a big response, seeing young lives changed and transformed more into the likeness of Jesus. The regular youth event is core business and really is one of the peak experiences of the week. But when it comes to the faith formation and discipleship of young people, it is not enough. A youth event on its own will not grow disciples that last. It helps but it is not enough. It is just the beginning.

On the other side of the coin, if we focus only on the journey of a young person we come up short. Crafting meaningful shared experiences for young people to engage with is vital. For example, life groups and community building times are both essential. If done well, the regular youth night can go beyond the 'main event' to create a sense of community and gathered experience that can intersect with the ongoing journey of a young person. It is here, often in the smaller relational group, that God breaks in, His redemptive work gets traction and honest conversations are had.

Effective discipleship occurs in a rich environment that is both 'event' and 'journey' orientated. This is found in fun and meaningful youth events, underpinned by life groups, and significant adults being present in the lives of young people, leading them through the tricky adolescent years. This big rock needs to go first if we are to effectively care for and reach the next generation.

Big themes and ideas can be taught at the main event and then unpacked and made personal in a life group with a leader asking questions. The leader will really care for and know the story of each young person in the group. Lots of fun can be had in big group games at the start of the evening, but deeper community grows out of conversations that happen later in the evening during supper and hang-time.

Consider how Jesus navigated this territory. He spent time in big groups feeding the five thousand and teaching the Sermon on the Mount. He also walked the path with the twelve and had many personal interactions of significance along the journey, such as the woman at the well and the healing of Jairus's daughter.[10] Jesus valued the event but also knew that engaging in the journey of his followers was important. It is not event or journey, but event *and* journey.

How much time do you spend on the event? Is your calendar full of tasks to be completed for youth group, or is it balanced with interactions in the lives of youth and leaders, growing an ongoing culture of faith development?

JESUS VALUED THE EVENT BUT ALSO KNEW THAT ENGAGING IN THE JOURNEY OF HIS FOLLOWERS WAS IMPORTANT.

[10] Feeding the five thousand (Luke 9); Sermon on the Mount (Matthew 5-7); Woman at the Well (John 4); Healing of Jairus's daughter (Mark 5).

DISCIPLE-MAKING PATHWAYS

You did not choose me, but I chose you and appointed you so that you might go and bear fruit—fruit that will last—and so that whatever you ask in my name the Father will give you.[11]

Jesus tells us that as we abide in Him we will bear fruit that will last. The ministry essentials of love, reach, grow and multiply[12] create a pathway for an effective youth ministry. They are vital ingredients in bearing fruit that will last and grow, producing a ministry that makes disciples who make disciples. As we plan this first, other important ministry pursuits can go in around them.

Let's unpack each of these essentials.

Love

Love people both locally and globally. In youth ministry, this means providing many opportunities for youth to engage in restoring our world. From serving in a local soup kitchen to taking teams of students overseas on mission trips, having a

---

[11] John 15: 16

[12] Pastor Dale Stephenson, Crossway Baptist Church, Australia, 2010.

youth ministry that loves the world is essential. This reflects Jesus' heart for service and mission. Does your youth ministry show genuine love and care for people in your local neighbourhood? What about globally?

Reach

Have a plan to share Jesus with the community. It may be through schools, coaching, student outreach or something else. Having a culture of reaching out and taking risks to see people come to know Jesus is essential. Reach initiatives keep the ministry outward focused and help make disciples. Do you have a pathway in reaching the youth in your local area? Are you seeing people come to know Jesus through this strategy? What is one thing you could change to give more young people from your local area the opportunity to come to know Jesus?

Grow

Have a strategy to equip and empower youth for the mission of making disciples. This includes a clear focus on discipleship pathways and relational discipleship, mobilising and training volunteer leaders, partnering with parents and families, and working to foster effective community. The grow pathway is mostly about the empowering and mobilising of those who already know Jesus, to be equipped in sharing their faith with others in an authentic and real way. Creating an environment for sharing and accountability is essential here. What fruit are you seeing of young people growing with Jesus? Are you baptising young people? Are you hearing stories of them sharing their faith at school?

Multiply

Be ready to push beyond the comfort zone to grow and multiply the ministry for the sake of God's Kingdom. Multiplication is a key ministry essential in seeing young people love their world, reach their friends for Jesus, and grow in their faith. If they are loving, reaching and growing, then multiplying is the natural outworking of such behaviours. The Christian bubble can be a safe place to live and it is the leaders' challenge to set a culture of multiplication.

I have been involved in multiplying a youth ministry from Year 7 to 12 to Juniors (yrs 7-9) and Seniors (yrs 10-12) so that we could be more age specific and be smaller in size. As we were more age specific, we started to see young people invite their friends. The groups being smaller made it easier for young people to be known in community. Due to multiplying the ministry, we grew in seeing young people come to know Jesus and also grew in deeper community. What do you need to multiply in your ministry so that more people can be reached for the Kingdom?

Pastor Dale Stephenson calls the love, reach, grow and multiply pathway, the "irreducible minimum"[13] of effective discipleship. Each ministry essential is a big rock that is vital in creating a pathway for relational discipleship.

If you are honest, where does the pathway of your ministry lead? What fruit are you experiencing? What could the pathway of love, reach, grow, multiply look like in your ministry?

EACH MINISTRY ESSENTIAL IS A BIG ROCK
THAT IS A VITAL IN CREATING A PATHWAY FOR
RELATIONAL DISCIPLESHIP.

[13] Pastor Dale Stephenson, 2010.

BIG ROCK 6:

MULTIPLY YOURSELF

As I sit and listen to emerging leaders, I don't hear them crying out for more teaching or the latest book to read (except this one of course!). They have the means to access that information. What I do hear, is that they crave *proximity* to excellent leaders, usually older than themselves, to help them grow and be equipped.

I believe one of the big challenges facing us right now is the need to develop the next generation of leaders, who are willing and ready to take on a new wave of significant leadership roles.

Jesus' approach to building leaders was a layered, life-on-life method with a potent blend of theory and practice. Jesus taught and cared for the masses. For example, feeding the five thousand[14] and preaching the Sermon on the Mount.[15] He trained up the seventy-two and sent them out two by two.[16] He called and trained a smaller group, the twelve, calling them by name to be with him[17], doing life-on-life with them, and giving them specific

[14] Matthew 14: 13-21

[15] Matthew 5-7

[16] Luke 10: 1-12

[17] Mark 3: 14

ministry assignments.[18] He also went deeper and poured into the three: Peter, James and John. They had extra access to the private world and thoughts of King Jesus. Examples of this include the Garden of Gethsemane[19], the transfiguration[20], and the healing of Jairus's daughter.[21]

I love what Michael Hyatt says:

"After interacting with leaders on every level for more than 3 decades, my observation is that most leaders only focus on the first two strategies (masses and 72). They have a public teaching ministry and are good at mobilising groups for specific assignments. However, very few intentionally train a small group of disciples. Even fewer build deep relationships with a handful of confidants. As a result, they do not have the kind of lasting impact they could have."[22]

As leaders, each one of us has been built into along our journey. But it should not stop there. **We need to have a commitment to multiply that investment, not only to the masses and to the**

[18] Mark 3: 14-15

[19] Luke 22:39-46

[20] Matthew 17: 1-14

[21] Luke 8:51

[22] Michael Hyatt, "The Leadership Strategy of Jesus", Michael Hyatt Blog, March 24, 2010, http://michaelhyatt.com/the-leadership-strategy-of-jesus.html, accessed 14/4/2017.

seventy-two, but to the twelve and especially to the three. I believe we are being built into, to build into others. At the core of Jesus' leadership development approach was relationship and multiplication. You could say He did his best work with a few. Therefore, this needs to be at the heart of our discipleship and leadership development.

As we raise up the emerging generation, it's my personal conviction that our need is not for more programs (we have enough great development vehicles in play). Our need is for more leaders investing into new leaders' lives. This is a big rock in effective youth ministry and therefore it needs to go first. You and I can most effectively equip the next generation of leaders by pulling them in close and teaching them, life-on-life, like Jesus did.

Will you embrace this paradigm of going deeper with a few? Will you go beyond equipping the masses and the seventy-two, and give big chunks of your time to developing the twelve and the three? Can you name the emerging leaders on your radar into whose lives you can proactively invest?

Does anyone else remember the glue you used in pre-school? If yours was anything like mine, it was thick, clumpy and probably edible! Yet as I look back at my scrapbooks, I can't help but notice my beautiful paper creations are rapidly peeling off. The problem with this glue…*it doesn't stick!*

Relationship is the glue of ministry. We might agree with this, we might even articulate it, but do our practices, programs and priorities actually reflect this truth? Some of us will be discovering this glue for the first time, for others it will be a matter of upgrading the pre-school glue to something stronger. Either way, let's ensure that our glue sticks by putting our insights into practice!

When I reflect on the Big Rocks of youth ministry, even as someone who has been immersed in these insights for some time, they continue to challenge me. How easy it is to slip back into being program-centric and event-orientated when immediate results are what our society celebrates. And let's be honest, it gives us a good feeling as well. Programs and events are easy to "sell" to our ministry supervisor or congregation, and often seem to validate our role. To lead by example, build relationships, and to think long-term requires significant sacrifice.

Take a moment to consider your context and ask yourself –
as I seek to place these Big Rocks in first **what are the forces
working against me right now?**

- A lack of time

- A lack of volunteers

- We celebrate the wrong things

- My role will be at risk

Other

When I first arrived at Stirling Theological College in 2007, I
quickly realised that were very few people like me; young rural
guys who felt called to ministry straight out of school. The range
of experiences I had over the next few years were amazing, and
yet my formative years as a Youth Pastor and strategic leader
were most definitely under the leadership of Mike at Crossway
Baptist Church. He would regularly talk with the team about
"discipleship edges" and "relational spaces" with such passion
and conviction that I knew it was going to stick. These concepts
gave language to my instinct, and his own investment in me was
evidence enough that relational discipleship was, and remains,
the path forward.

I vividly recall one specific moment as I considered what it would take to truly embrace a relational model of ministry. Sitting at an empty table in the church café, I remember thinking to myself, "If we are going to make this happen, we will need to double our leadership" – a very intimidating thought! Activity is fleeting, but true impact takes courage, a plan, and patience.

Yet even in the face of challenge I cannot deny that relationship is the glue. While I may recall a specific camp experience or a word of encouragement spoken over me, at the end of the day it is *names* that I remember. That camp experience was a *shared* experience, that word of encouragement was delivered via a *person* whom I trusted. Is it any wonder that every youth leader I have ever recruited or trained, I compare to Phil, my own youth leader?

MAKE THE GLUE STICK

1. To grow the culture of relational discipleship within my ministry context, **which one** (or two MAX) **of the six Big Rocks do I need to prioritise right now?**

Follow Your Calling	Disciple Making Pathways
Event and Journey	Relational Currency
People > Programs	Multiply Yourself

2. **Who do I need to chat with** in order to gain momentum or overcome resistance as I prioritise this?

☐   my supervisor

☐   an external mentor

☐   my team

☐   my former Youth Leader

☐   my Lead Pastor

Other

3. **Send them a text message right now.** "Hey [Person]. I've recently been reading about this idea of [Big Rock] and would love your insights. Could we arrange a time to catch up and chat about it?"

☐   Message sent

☐   The person is sitting next to me

Ministry that centres around relationship is inevitably and necessarily full of risk. We, along with our leaders, will reproduce who we are, the good and the bad. All the more reason to be deliberate about our direction!

NEXT STEP

THINK	ACT
In which of our current ministry programs would we find it easiest to elevate people over program?	Chat with my supervisor about including a "development" outcome in my position description.
If I want to set an example, who am I currently investing relationally in?	Make more deliberate relational deposits or withdrawals.
How as a team do we measure success?	Recruit more team members.

LEADING YOURSELF

Bill George, in his book *Discover Your True North* says, "The hardest person you will ever have to lead is yourself."[23] Would you agree? I believe this statement to be true. Self leadership is absolutely crucial in being an effective human being and therefore an effective leader in God's Kingdom. Being an authentic disciple of Jesus Christ means having a learning posture and being willing to look in the mirror at yourself and self reflect before looking out the window and leading others.[24]

---

[23] Bill George, *Discover Your True North: Becoming an Authentic Leader* (New Jersey, USA: John Wiley & Sons, 2015), 7.

[24] Jim Collins, 33-35.

Section 2 will focus on leading yourself, exploring the following insights:

1: *STAY CLOSE TO JESUS*

2: *REST AND RECHARGE*

3: *LEADERS DO THE UNCOMFORTABLE*

4: *LEADING WITH HUMILITY*

5: *THREE WAYS TO BE A LIFELONG LEARNER*

6: *TURNING LEARNING INTO ACTION*

7: *WHAT IS YOUR LENS?*

STAY CLOSE TO JESUS

I met with a young leader from a local youth ministry who asked how he could get better at answering questions put forward by his year seven boys. He often felt stuck and was uncertain how to proceed.

This raised a little alarm bell in me, so I chased the noise and asked him how his own spiritual formation and practices were going. He shared that he struggled to find a rhythm and a regular approach to his relationship with Jesus.

In several years of leading young people and young adults, I have found this to be very common. If what I've described sounds like you, or is true for the people you lead, don't feel bad. We all experience ups and downs in our personal rhythm with God. I believe that a healthy relationship with God is the most important thing to have, so don't give up on it. Let me encourage you to prioritise your personal relationship with Jesus, and lead from this place.

Andy Stanley's father told him that the "most important thing in your life is your relationship with Jesus!"[25] No argument from me there. In *Eat this Book*, Eugene Peterson says, "The Christian scriptures are the primary text for Christian spirituality."[26]

Staying close to Jesus means getting into the Bible, so here are three tips I've learnt from others who have walked this road longer than me.[27]

1. Time

Have a regular time to read the Bible. Some are early morning people (not me!) and some are night owls (not really me either!). Find a time that works for you. For me, it's first thing over breakfast. I find it helps me calibrate and get into the right space for the coming day.

2. Place

Have a place where you open the Bible. It could be your bedroom, or lounge, a park bench, the toilet or breakfast table. I don't care

[25] Andy Stanley, *Deep and Wide: Creating Churches Unchurched People Love to Attend* (Grand Rapids, Michigan: Zondervan, 2012), 117.

[26] Eugene Peterson, *Eat this Book: The Art of Spiritual Reading* (London, UK: Hodder & Stoughton, 2008), 15.

[27] Pastor Karl Faase taught the principles of "T, P, M" at an Arrow Australia emerging leaders' residential in 2010.

where it is, as long as you have a regular place that will act like a trigger in your mind to remind you to open the Bible when you are there. This is helpful in building healthy habits for your spiritual formation. My place currently is the breakfast bar. The Bible sits on it and I am reminded each morning to pick it up and read.

3. Method

Okay, so you have a time and a place. Now you need a method. How will you explore the transforming Word of our living God? There are multiple options to help you regularly read and digest God's Word.

- YouVersion app – Bible reading plans.

- YouVersion app – Bible audio.

- Alternating your daily readings in a set rhythm, such as OT book, Gospel, NT book, Gospel, OT book, Gospel, NT book, etc.

- Using a printed Bible reading plan, such as *Everyday with Jesus* or *Search the Scriptures.*

- Dwelling in a passage or book for a longer period, perhaps using Lectio Divina or the SOAP method (Scripture, Observation, Application, Prayer).

When it comes to leading yourself, the most important thing is to stay close to Jesus. Leading from your growing relationship with Him is essential for effective ministers of the gospel. As you do this remember T, P, M – time, place and method.

How do you get into the Bible? What time, place and method works best for you?

REST AND RECHARGE

In Australia, Christmas is a busy time. Ministry calendars tend to be packed with final youth nights, leaders' celebrations, Christmas shows, Christmas services, and the list goes on. This is all good and we need to embrace it. But, when we hit Boxing Day, there is generally an opportunity to rest up and recharge for the year to come. I usually take an extended break over late December and early January. Whether you take a long break over summer or at some other time of the year, here are two things I encourage you to do:

1. Disconnect

Be intentional about disconnecting from technology and work. For me this means no checking of emails and no checking in on social media to see what others are up to. I find I just get sucked back into the work world and get so easily distracted.

I know my workplace want me to rest and they are not asking me to work on my break, so I need to resist the urge to check in on things. Sometimes the distinction between work and life can be fuzzy and the lines aren't always clear, so to avoid temptations or distractions over summer, I've found it helpful to disconnect my email exchange and delete social media apps off my phone.

2. Reconnect

Aim to be especially present with family and friends over your holiday break. Even if you feel connected with them already, when taking a break it's a great opportunity to reconnect at a deeper level through quality time. As I disconnect and my body and soul find rest, I am intentional about reconnecting with family and friends. All of this reconnection time builds life and creates a platform of relationship for the year ahead.

As I look at the gospels and study the life of Jesus, I see a man who worked out of rhythms of grace. He had an incredible flow to His life that teaches us much about disconnecting and reconnecting. He worked hard but also rested hard, and His work always came out of His rest with His Father.

How will you disconnect on your next long break? Who do you need to reconnect with during your next holiday?

LEADERS DO THE UNCOMFORTABLE

When was the last time you did something uncomfortable? I don't mean wearing skinny jeans, walking the stairs instead of taking the lift, or running a half marathon! As a leader in God's Kingdom, when was the last time you were out on the edge, feeling uncomfortable for Him?

As church leaders, living in the uncomfortable zone should be common for us. Whether it is taking the initiative to meet new people, trying new projects to see people come to know Jesus, or creating positive cultures in our ministry areas to grow the church, being stretched is part of leading yourself.

Paul challenges us on how to live as we put ourselves out on the edge for Jesus. Here is a perspective check from 2 Corinthians 6:

We put no stumbling block in anyone's path, so that our ministry will not be discredited. Rather, as servants of God we commend ourselves in every way: in great endurance; in troubles, hardships and distresses; in beatings, imprisonments and riots; in hard work, sleepless nights and hunger; in purity, understanding, patience and kindness; in the Holy Spirit and in sincere love; in truthful speech and in the power of God; with weapons of righteousness in the right hand and in the left; through glory and dishonour, bad report and good report; genuine, yet regarded as impostors; known, yet regarded as unknown; dying, and yet we live on; beaten, and yet not killed; sorrowful, yet always rejoicing; poor, yet making many rich; having nothing, and yet possessing everything. We have spoken freely to you, Corinthians, and *opened wide our hearts to you. We are not withholding our affection from you, but you are withholding yours from us. As a fair exchange—I speak as to my children— open wide your hearts* also.[28]

[28] 2 Corinthians 6:3-13

Wow! Paul lays out what it looks like to live in the uncomfortable zone. In his ministry he put no stumbling block in anyone's path, lived for Jesus through trials and hardships, and opened his heart wide to the people God brought across his path. He embraced the uncomfortable things and led his teams accordingly so that many could have the opportunity to come to know Jesus.

Paul's message to the Corinthians is applicable to us today. We can easily fold into ourselves rather than being outward-focused. We gravitate towards what is comfortable rather than embracing the uncomfortable. It is a great blessing to be part of a church community that is willing to be uncomfortable for the sake of the gospel. Let's be challenged, as Paul says, and open our hearts wide to all God has for us.

How are you living in the uncomfortable zone? What is one step you can take today, this day, to be uncomfortable for the sake of the gospel?

LEADING WITH HUMILITY

Recently I had an experience that really tested my leadership skills.

I had to navigate a difficult pastoral situation between two families, which required me to discern the truth and speak some tough but very important words. This was a complex and multi-layered situation. After it had all been worked through, and a pastoral care plan was put in place, I realised I failed to follow up with one set of parents.

Once I was alerted to this by someone above me in the organisation, I set up a meeting with the parents. When we met, my opening line was to ask about the young person. Upon reflection, my opening line should have been an apology.

Two fails by me.

The next day I sent an email apologising to the parents concerned. I validated their concerns, renewed our ministry's partnership with their family and spoke of the preferred future of seeing their young person growing in their faith.

This was a big lesson for me. As an experienced Youth Pastor, I had dealt with conflict previously, but I was challenged to keep a soft heart and lead with humility. **Humility is a core ingredient of leadership. It is essential to have a soft heart, an open mind and a willingness to accept your failings and move forward.** So, next time (I hope there won't be a next time, but I am a realist) I find myself in a similar situation I am going to remember to lead with an apology that sets the tone for the rest of the conversation.

Where in your life or ministry do you need to lead with humility? Who do you need to speak with, apologise to or renew your commitment with?

THREE WAYS TO BE A LIFELONG LEARNER

I recently had lunch with one of our up and coming leaders and we chatted at length about life and leadership. For nearly two hours we explored the hot topics of life and ministry and I loved every moment of it! As we chatted I felt I was being refreshed and I learnt so much through the conversation. As you consider leading yourself, here are three big ideas I gained from my lunch meeting:

1. Grow into the calling God has for your life

As emerging leaders, we simply don't *arrive*. We are constantly growing in capacity and often learning through the pain of our mistakes. God knows this and He wants to keep growing us and enlarging our capacity. It is essential for us to grow into our calling, in the same way that many of us have grown into adulthood. Cut yourself some slack, create a grace space for growth and make sure you have the right people walking alongside you to help keep you focused and on track.

2. Develop a sustainable work-life rhythm with margin

Work-life balance is dead. If you are trying to balance your life like trying to balance weights on scales, you will never get it right. Two key words for me are rhythm and margin. Create a sustainable rhythm. When you work hard, make sure you rest hard as well. Understand the seasons of life and don't always have the throttle on full. Build margin into your day and don't always have meetings back to back. In my diary, I usually allow one and a half hours for a one hour meeting, to give a small margin in case the meeting goes over time or I need some extra time to prepare for my next meeting. Obviously, there are days and seasons when this is hard to achieve, but let it be your aspiration.

3. Value theological training

If you desire to be in ministry long term, don't ignore theological training and ongoing spiritual formation. Make sure you choose the right college (some research is needed here) and take your calling seriously by gaining extra training. I believe it's not enough to learn only from your pastor or local church. You need a broader experience: one that is robust enough to grow and shake your faith, for you to own some real truths in your life. This will also help you grow into your calling.

What is one thing you need to focus on to become a lifelong learner?

TURNING LEARNING INTO ACTION

When you listen to a sermon, hear a podcast or go to a conference, how do you translate your learning into action? Sometimes we can be rich with information and have the best of intentions to make changes in multiple areas of our lives, but then we forget or move on to the next thing that needs our attention. Part of leading yourself is turning learning into action. So, how can we make the leap from information to action?

When my brain is full of new information, and I have lots of thoughts and big ideas, to ground my vision and move from information to action I use this simple, three questions framework.

1. What can I do this week to bring change?

Here I am looking for a simple opportunity to clarify what God has been saying to me and to start the change process. Often this is personal and something I need to wrestle through with God or my family.

2. What can I do this month to bring change?

This is an achievable step that might take a little more time to set up: for example, a strategic meeting with your leader or wider church team. Here I am thinking about a mid-term implementation of what God has said. I name it this way to allow time to set myself and my broader team up for a win.

3. What can I do this year to bring change?

Here I am thinking about longer term and more cultural change. This is the kind of big idea that could really make a huge impact if the key stakeholders engage in its implementation. Here I am asking God for a little window into the future and asking if this will really add value to our mission of making disciples.

In all of this we need accountability. I know that if I am to stick to the vision, then I need to share my ideas with someone who will ask how I'm going in moving towards them.

Next time you learn, ask these three simple questions and move from information to action.

WHAT IS YOUR LENS?

We all have a lens that causes us to see life and the world we live in, in a certain way. This is known as our worldview.

I vividly remember meeting with a local Youth Pastor. He shared with me how he had read about a great idea and was ready to implement it then and there. It was significant and would represent a big change in his ministry. So, I asked him to consider how it fitted into the bigger picture of his ministry. This opened up a conversation on why we do what we do. This conversation showed me how important it is to understand the way we process new ideas and information. How we lead ourselves through this process is crucial in our overall leadership success. If we cannot lead ourselves in this way we won't be able to effectively lead others.

Let me propose four lenses I use when considering a new ministry idea:

1. Ministry Context

All of our ministries exist within a context: the socio-economic status of our families, the education levels of the youth, and their family background, to name just a few. These factors need to be considered when thinking about new ideas. For example, will the idea be too expensive? Will it impact senior high youth when they are studying for exams? Putting your idea through the lens of your ministry context will instantly tell you whether or not you should pursue it any further.

2. Best Practice

Using the lens of best practice gives you confidence to trust past trends and future hopes to see if your idea carries weight. You need to ask these questions. What are you doing that's working / not working? What does past experience teach you? What are you reading that affirms or discounts the idea? Who are you listening to? What are you hearing from trusted others?

3. God at Work

As you look around your church and local community, where do you see God already at work? Let me push you with a further question. How can you join Him in this work? When I was chatting to the same Youth Pastor I asked him this question. He began to tell me about all the cool stuff his local council was doing for young people, so I challenged him, how can you join this work? Partnerships can pop up all over the place if we are open to them.

The lens of 'God at work' provides a great foundation for future ideas and initiatives.

4. What Are You Hearing from God?

Deep in your heart when you still yourself before Jesus, what is He telling you is the next step in your ministry? With an attentive ear for the Holy Spirit, where are you being challenged? **Intimacy with Jesus and obedience to Him is the most important lens.** So, make sure you have lots of time with Jesus, listening to what He is saying. Andy Stanley says we need to marry the mission (of making disciples) but date the method.[29] So if the method is negotiable, we need the lens of intimacy with Jesus to have the discernment to know which way to go.

Next time you read or hear about a great new ministry initiative and want to make a change, think about putting the idea through these different lenses.

What is your youth ministry lens? How do you see the youth ministry world and why do you do what you do?

---

[29] Andy Stanley, 284.

Leading yourself keeps the glue sticky. One of the things that I always appreciated about Mike's leadership was the way he continually drew us back to the need to invest in our own spiritual lives: celebrating God's work on our character development came first. In demanding ministry contexts, it was far too easy to get busy, and in the process, lose that essential connection to Jesus, despite His encouragement (or is it a warning?) that *"apart from me you can do nothing"* (John 15:5). Great leaders *will* produce great programs, but that cannot be the primary desired outcome, rather, I have discovered, it is collateral benefit of walking closely with our Creator.

When it comes to leading ourselves, I've been reminded that the greatest characteristic for us to embody is that of teachability. To be teachable is to embrace a deeply humble posture. It reverses the compulsion of my mouth to speak, and forces my ears to open to the infinite and providential resources that God has placed around me. I'm not sure if it is a common practice among pastors, but I regularly reflect on who I once was, what I once thought, believed, even shared, and marvel at the fact that God would choose to use me. If you need a reminder on the importance of being teachable, pull out the notes of your first sermon, *I dare you.*

Why don't you take a moment to think back to who you were five years ago. **What is one of the most important lessons you have learnt since then, and who did you learn it from?**

	The Lesson	Who I Listened To
1.		
2.		

We are all a work in progress, and the sooner we learn that, the better.

An essential prerequisite to leading ourselves is *understanding* ourselves. The importance of healthy rest and the opportunity to recharge resonates with me deeply. Something that I committed to from the early days of my ministry was to embrace the practice of Sabbath. For me, this meant taking a day a week where I did no church-related work whatsoever. Even at a young age I had seen too many leaders burn-out through self-dependence or an inability to maintain boundaries, and I certainly knew that it was going to be a risk for me. Sabbath was a concept that flew in the face of what society expected and yet by doing this, it granted me access to a new level of leadership that I would never have been able to experience had it not been for the discipline associated with such a step.

It starts with us. If we are to take seriously the call to lead and disciple others, we need to ensure that we provide the best example possible for those under our care to imitate. Contrary perhaps to Christian instinct, to invest in yourself is not selfish, it's essential.

MAKE THE GLUE STICK

1. What area of leadership do I need to **prioritise right now?**

   ▫ **Growing in Character** ▫ **Growing in Competency**

2. Which of the specific lessons within this section do I need to work on the most?

(Title) ______________________________

3. Time for a **quick health check**. If I were to take a snapshot of the last three months, where would I mark myself on each of these continuums?

Spiritually Empty   Spiritually Full

← - →

Physically Exhausted   Physically Refreshed

← - →

Emotionally Distraught   Emotionally Balanced

← - →

4. Are there any changes I need to make to lead myself better? Who do I need to speak to?

☐   my supervisor

☐   my team

☐   an external mentor

☐   my Lead Pastor

(Send them a text message right now.)

Leadership is always a work in progress, and too often feels like reformation even as we crave revolution. Yet authenticity does not require completion, and honesty of the journey is exactly what we want those who follow us to imitate.

THINK	ACT
Is there anyone I need to apologise to? Is there an apology that I have been putting off?	Establish a devotional rhythm for yourself (daily prayer, bible reading)
What aspect of ministry have I been doing in my own strength, "apart" from Jesus?	Take a retreat day or weekend away.
Am I a teachable person? In what context do I need to listen more and speak less?	Pursue some additional theological training

LEADING OTHERS

Leadership guru John Maxwell states, "Great leaders produce other leaders."[30] The development of trained and effective leaders is essential in fulfilling Jesus' Great Commission to go into all the world to make multiplying disciples. Put simply: leading others matters!

In the coming years, we may have a leadership vacuum in our nation as baby boomers retire and exit the workforce. Producing effective, gospel-orientated leaders needs to be a priority. It is not good enough to have leaders who can run a great program but are lacking in character and the ability to select, recruit, train, equip and release others.

---

[30] John Maxwell, *Developing The Leaders Around You: How to help Others Reach Their Full Potential* (Nashville, USA: Thomas Nelson, 1995), 3.

Section 3 will explore the following insights with a focus on leading others:

1: *REPRODUCTION, EMPOWERMENT AND MOBILISATION*

2: *LESSONS FOR YOUTH MINISTRY GROWTH*

3: *LEADING EFFECTIVE CHANGE*

4: *THE FOUR BIG ASKS OF YOUTH LEADERSHIP*

5: *WE FOCUS ON WHAT WE MEASURE*

6: *COMMUNICATION IS KEY*

7: *RECRUITING THE RIGHT KIND OF LEADER*

8: *TEAM RETREATS*

9: *LAST QUARTER CONVERSATIONS*

REPRODUCTION, EMPOWERMENT AND MOBILISATION

I'm convinced that a leader's most crucial task is to reproduce themselves. I'm not alone in this belief. Many leading thinkers and practitioners argue in favour of leadership multiplication.

Missional leadership expert Mike Breen's approach to developing leaders comes from two main assumptions: one, you reproduce who you are, and two, leaders define culture.[31]

Leadership guru Robert Clinton says, "A major function of all leadership is that of selection of rising leadership. Leaders must continually be aware of God's processing of younger leaders and work with that processing."[32]

Peter Corney writes on the development of leaders being key to the future of the church. He says, "The future of any organisation

---

[31] Mike Breen, *Multiplying Missional Leaders: From Half-Hearted Volunteers to a Mobilised Kingdom Force* (Pawleys Island, USA: 3dm, 2012), 98.

[32] Robert Clinton, *The Making of a Leader: Recognising the Lessons and Stages of Leadership Development* (Colorado Springs, USA: NavPress, 2012), 182.

lies in its ability to reproduce leaders of quality."[33] He also explains that if your vision is for one year, plant wheat. If your vision is for ten years, plant trees. But, if your vision is for a lifetime, plant people.[34]

Leadership expert John Maxwell says the following about leadership reproduction. "True success comes only when every generation continues to develop the next generation."[35] He asks, "Who will take your place? There is no success without a successor."[36]

In his famous book *Spiritual Leadership*, J Oswald Sanders quotes John R Mott. "Leaders must multiply themselves by developing younger leaders, giving them full play and adequate outlet for their abilities. Younger people should feel the weight of heavy burdens, opportunity for initiative, and power of the final decision. The younger leader should receive generous credit for achievements. Foremost they must be trusted. Blunders are the inevitable price of training new leaders."[37]

[33] *Peter Corney, A Passion For Leadership: Insights From Arrow Australia Leadership Team* (Kirrawee, NSW: Arrow Leadership Australia, 2009), 1.

[34] Peter Corney, 1.

[35] John Maxwell, 188.

[36] John Maxwell, 10.

[37] J. Oswald Sanders, *Spiritual Leadership* (Chicago, USA: Moody Press, 1994), 147.

In 2 Timothy 2:2 Paul says to his younger emerging leader, Timothy, "The things you have heard me say in the presence of many witnesses, entrust to reliable people who will also be qualified to teach others."

Recently I was meeting with a younger pastor and the conversation turned to the question of what constitutes effective ministry amongst young people. We chatted about a few different things, including the importance of a leader in reproducing themselves into the next generation. I shared with him what I believe to be four important words in shaping a healthy youth ministry. They are: Empowered Leaders, Mobilised Students. These four words embody the leaders' one task of reproducing themselves into their leaders and young people.

Growing a strong leadership team that is empowered to love Jesus, love students and serve by using their own initiative is an important building block in a healthy ministry. **Developing and empowering leaders and multiplying yourself into others must be an essential goal of any aspiring leader.** You can only lead so far and be in one place at a time, therefore, growing your ministry footprint by building into others is crucial.

Mobilising your students into mission is the other important building block. They are on the front line of schools, sporting clubs, part-time workplaces, etc. As you invest in and disciple them, both in corporate teaching and in smaller life groups, always keep the mission of God central to all you do. Youth group is a great place for teaching, community and bringing friends along, but students must also be equipped to live out their faith in their own mission fields, where they spend most of their time.

Who are you investing in? How are you reproducing yourself? How does your calendar reflect this being a priority in your ministry?

How can you take the four words, Empowered Leaders, Mobilised Students, into your ministry, so that your leaders can flourish and your students are on mission?

LESSONS FOR YOUTH MINISTRY GROWTH

I'm often asked, "How do you grow a youth ministry?" As leaders, we all pray and seek God, try to build a team, and generally do our best with what God has given us. Beyond the basics, here are my top five key lessons for growing a youth ministry.

1. Structure for Growth

I don't buy clothes for my kids that are too small; I buy them with space so they can grow. It's exactly the same in youth ministry. We need to structure it for growth. It is essential to have a solid structure that utilises gifts and talents, and facilitates growth. Jesus had a structure: from the masses, to the seventy-two, to his twelve and then the inner circle of three. Be sure to involve all stakeholders (parents, youth, local schools, etc.) in the conversation of structure, so that together you can achieve more. Mike Breen says, "creating simple repeatable patterns"[38] is key to making and multiplying disciples. How can your structure help facilitate this?

---

[38] Mike Breen, tour of Australia, 2013.

2. To Get Bigger, It Needs to Get Smaller

Life groups are an engine for growth because they are where youth are known and stories are shared. It is my belief that big events need to be accompanied by healthy life groups. I tell my life group leaders they are the Youth Pastor to the youth they lead. Initially this freaks them out, but they gain insight into the importance of their role in the youth team.

We surveyed our youth[39] and the results showed that they invite friends to youth group in this order: first to an outreach night, second to a life group night and third to a gathering / service night. Consequently, we have life groups each fortnight to develop relational connection between young people, making the big group smaller.

3. Be Outcome Orientated

Inevitably, we focus on what we measure. So let me ask you, what do you measure? Is it the ABC of growth: Attendance, Buildings, Cash? Or is it D for Disciples? If it's D, the question is how do you measure discipleship?

---

[39] I believe it's important to review your progress each year, by surveying all key stakeholders in some form.

In the ministry I lead, we measure key decisions made by a growing disciple: making a first time commitment, being baptised, being active in a life group, serving, and sharing their faith with others. You may need to review what is most effective in achieving the outcome you desire. Ask yourself or your team these two questions. What do we need to stop doing that is not effective? What do we need to start doing to become more effective? And keep in mind, "activity doesn't equal accomplishment."[40]

4. Be Clear About What You Ask from Volunteer Leaders

Are you clear, really clear, about what you are asking your leaders to do? I use the Four Big Asks of Youth Leadership (more on this later) as a useful tool for setting a baseline standard and empowering leaders to lead well. Our desire is to create a culture of leadership where every young person is cared for by a significant adult walking alongside them. For this to happen we need to be clear and intentional. When it happens well, watch this space because growth in your ministry will take off!

---

[40] Carey Nieuwhof speaking on church growth. See: http://careynieuwhof.com/8-reasons-most-churches-never-break-the-200-attendance-mark/#

5. Take Risks and Be Flexible

Vineyard movement founder John Wimber is widely regarded as being the originator of the saying: FAITH is spelt R-I-S-K. For growth to occur, the point leader needs to move out of the spotlight and create opportunities for others. Give the platform to up-and-comers (young leaders, youth) and continually try new initiatives to connect with the community. If in doubt, call it a pilot! Make a commitment to being flexible and to never stop innovating.

For this to work well, a culture needs to exist in the leadership team whereby "the best idea wins."[41] Regardless of where the idea comes from – Youth Pastor, the youngest youth group member or the freshest leader, the best idea wins!

If we posture ourselves as learners, as people who serve, and know that none of us have arrived, then we will see growth.

What do you do really well as a leader? If there was one thing you could change in yourself as a leader to see growth, what would it be?

---

[41] Pastor Dale Stephenson.

What do we do really well in growing a healthy youth ministry?

If there was one thing we could change about our ministry to see it grow, what would it be?

LEADING EFFECTIVE CHANGE

Spending regular time with Jesus asking the honest question, "How are we going, Lord?" should be a high priority for any leader. It's important to spend time reflecting on what is going well, what is not going well, and what needs to change. Not change for the sake of it, but in order to stay on the leading edge of loving God, loving people and making disciples.

I have been fortunate enough to have helped lead effective change in multiple organisations and in various roles. This is my simple framework for leading effective change.

Phase 1. Listening and Learning

Spend intentional time listening to and learning from the key stakeholders (staff, volunteers, families, local schools, etc). I call this: taking the pulse. In this phase I ask everyone the same three questions.

1. What's going really well that you love about [insert organisations name here]?

2. What concerns you and isn't going so well?

3. If you could change one thing, what would it be?

During this phase I have a notebook and madly write down all I can when meeting with people. With the volume of conversations that are had during this time, it's impossible to carry this much information in your mind.

Phase 2. Common Threads

You now have a notebook full of thoughts and you may have a sense of what God is saying through the body of Christ. It's time to spend some time in prayer discerning what God is saying. What are the common threads?

At this stage the change process needs to move from *you* as the leader, to *we* the community you are leading. It's really important to use inclusive language here. As you start to use *we*, ownership for change will build as people feel heard and acknowledged.

As you are discerning and praying, both individually and with your leadership team, ask these two questions.

1. What are some easy wins that could bring quick, effective change?

2. What are some longer term cultural changes that we believe God is speaking to us about?

Write down all your common threads as you listen to what God is saying.

Phase 3. Vision and Planning

Now is the time for some hard work as the change is prioritised into short, medium and long term goals. This needs to be done initially within the leadership team and then shared and developed with key stakeholders.

It is common in this phase to have multiple leadership vision planning nights, parent sessions and time shaping the intended change with highly invested young people. Be mindful not to swing the pendulum too far; just far enough to bring effective change. We are not seeking massive swings but marginal gains towards becoming more effective in our gospel outcomes.

It is also important to note that if you are going to say *yes* to something new, you might need to say *no* to something that's been around for a long time that is no longer fruitful. It is vital to be loving but ruthless during the planning phase. If you have executed the initial two phases well, you should have some relational currency to make the changes you need in phase three.

Phase 4. Roll Out

Now it is time to roll out the change. You just have to do it! This can be tricky because people like how it was. It's important to stay optimistic and keep speaking about the preferred future you desire. For example, "We are making this change for your friends who don't know Jesus yet."

Stay true to what God is asking of you, lean on your empowered and committed team for support, and make the change in a timely and effective manner.

As you roll out the change, make sure you over-communicate. Not everyone lives and breathes ministry, so some people might have missed the meetings or emails outlining the change and they might be caught off guard despite all your communication attempts. Show extra grace and be available for chats with parents or young people.

Phase 5. Ongoing Feedback Loops

The phrase "it's much easier to steer a moving ship" is so true. Once change is occurring and is no longer just theoretical, you can assess things more easily and continue to make effective alterations. After the first six months of any change it is important to have leader think tanks, student sessions and a parent night to gather feedback on how the change has rolled out.

This feedback will sharpen the effectiveness of the change and develop ownership from key stakeholders, increasing the chance for successful change. When people feel heard, they buy in. In this phase, it's important that the leader is not so invested in the change management process that they struggle to hear and receive honest feedback. How are you at receiving feedback?

To finish, let me encourage you that most people do want the best for their church. Some people struggle with change, so the goal of the leader needs to be to bring them along on the journey, and empower them in the process. In brief, remember this key leadership advice when leading change:

- Listen well. Don't be too precious. The truth is your friend.

- Involve all stakeholders in gathering feedback and information.

- Have a focus on empowering leaders. Let them feel the weight of change.

- Be committed to a structure that increases gospel outcomes.

- Be committed to the outcome and let your team embrace the process.

- As the point leader, you need to speak up and keep the vision of why the change is occurring at the forefront. Remember that not everyone lives and breathes ministry as much as we do!

What change do you need to lead in this or the coming season?

SOME PEOPLE STRUGGLE WITH CHANGE, SO THE GOAL OF THE LEADER NEEDS TO BE TO BRING THEM ALONG ON THE JOURNEY, AND EMPOWER THEM IN THE PROCESS.

THE FOUR BIG ASKS OF YOUTH LEADERSHIP

Sometimes I wonder if I really know what I am meant to do: as a husband, as a friend, in the leadership role I have at church, and even in life! If I cast my mind back to the first volunteer leader role I had leading a group of year eleven boys, at the time I had no idea what I was meant to do. I was so fresh it was scary! I remember sitting down with my pastor who talked me through the expectations and guidelines of youth leading. This was super helpful. My church also had a little booklet outlining the dos and don'ts of youth leading.

Over the years, I have wondered how well we set our volunteer leaders up for a win. Do we give them clear guidelines on what we are asking from them in youth leading? Most volunteer leaders ooze enthusiasm, have the right heart and love teenagers, but sometimes they have no idea what to do. At times, on youth group nights, little leader cliques emerge. This mostly happens because leaders can be fuzzy on what to do, so they fold into the safe space of chatting with their peers.

As a leader, I have wrestled with developing young leaders who are empowered to lead and not just do a task. I desire to see leaders who grow in authentic character and competency and who live a consistent life. This means that standards, expectations and a sense of clarity are important. But like most things, it is the way these are developed and delivered that is so critical.

I've moved away from exhaustive lists of guidelines and policies, as I feel they can become legalistic and unhelpful in the formation of a young leader's life. I've embraced a covenant approach[42] where, before God, the youth leadership team agree on what their lives stand for and why. This seems to help from a character perspective, but it still doesn't clarify what we are actually asking leaders to do.

To remedy this, I developed 'The Four Big Asks of Youth Leadership' to use as the basis of our leadership commitment and development. They are based around the journey and event nature of relational discipleship, looking to develop each leader to lead in a sustainable and holistic way. The next few pages will examine them one at a time.

---

[42] See Appendix 1 for an example of a Leader's Covenant

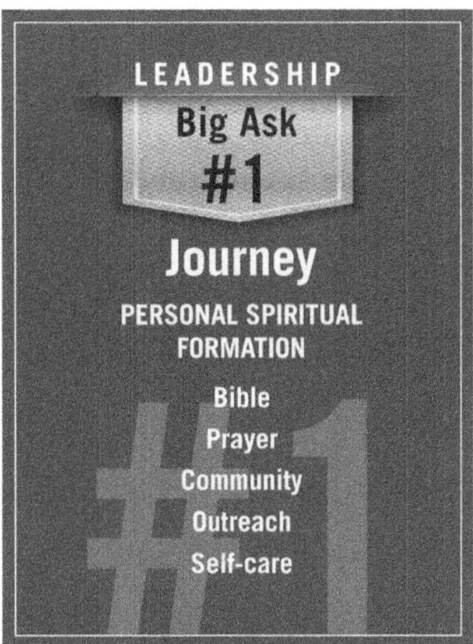
LEADERSHIP
Big Ask
#1
Journey
PERSONAL SPIRITUAL FORMATION
Bible
Prayer
Community
Outreach
Self-care
#1

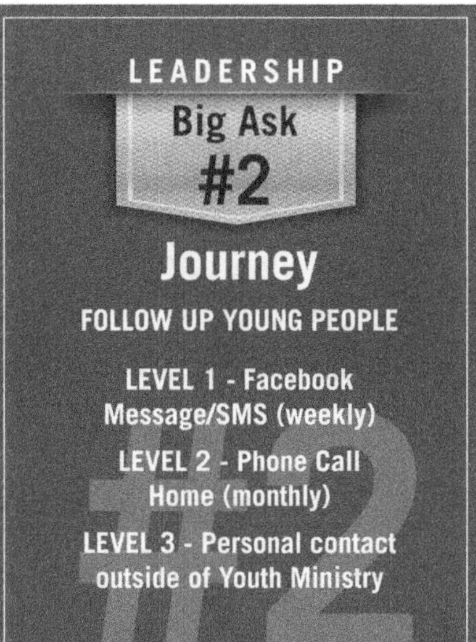
LEADERSHIP
Big Ask
#2
Journey
FOLLOW UP YOUNG PEOPLE
LEVEL 1 - Facebook Message/SMS (weekly)
LEVEL 2 - Phone Call Home (monthly)
LEVEL 3 - Personal contact outside of Youth Ministry
#2

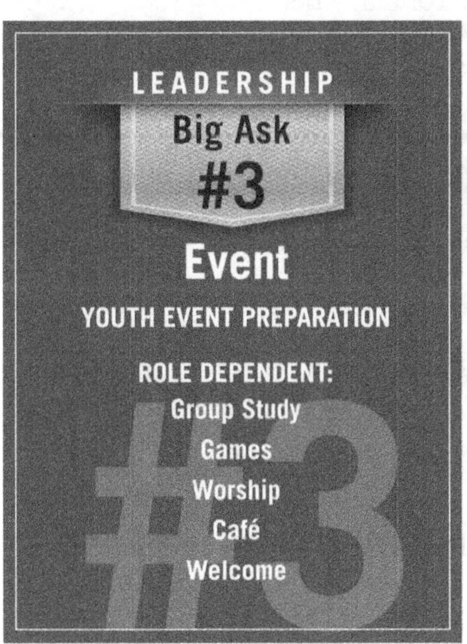
LEADERSHIP
Big Ask
#3
Event
YOUTH EVENT PREPARATION
ROLE DEPENDENT:
Group Study
Games
Worship
Café
Welcome
#3

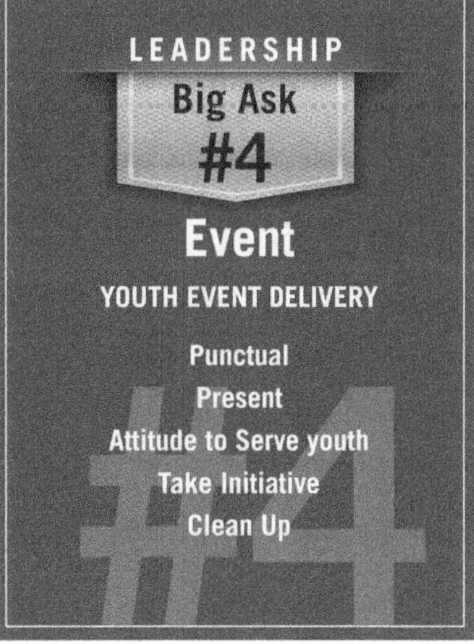
LEADERSHIP
Big Ask
#4
Event
YOUTH EVENT DELIVERY
Punctual
Present
Attitude to Serve youth
Take Initiative
Clean Up
#4

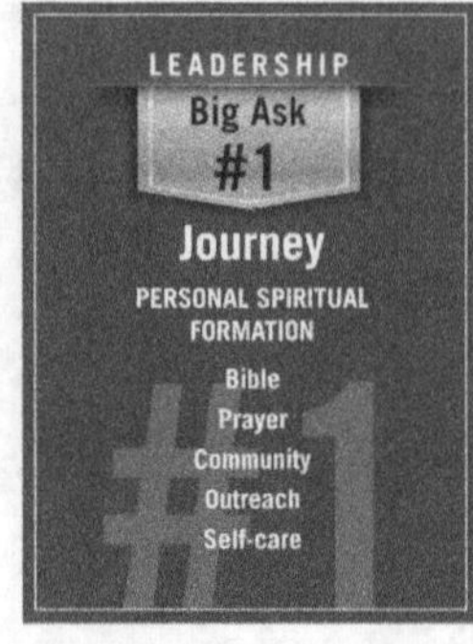

Big Ask #1: Lead from Your Growing Relationship with Jesus

There is so much to a role of youth leader: leading Bible studies, expert in gaming, professional wrestler, taxi driver, communicator, caterer, cleaner, the list goes on. When thinking about who to bring onto the team, it could be easy just to look at who can do what task. But that would be the wrong place to start. Character will always trump competency. It is important to get the right person on the team before you start to think about what their specific role may be.

Therefore, the first and most important 'Big Ask' is that leaders lead from their growing relationship with Jesus. A leader's personal spiritual formation and growth must be the basis and foundation of any leadership role. As a leader grows and wrestles with their personal faith and character formation, their own leadership develops.

The desire of my heart for youth leaders and for the culture we are seeking to grow, is to see authentic faith lived out in all the spaces and environments of our lives. This means regular engagement with the Bible, prayer, a life group, reaching out with the love of Jesus to their friends and family, and healthy self-care. This holistic approach aims to develop and nurture the leader as they in turn develop and nurture their youth. Youth leaders will be in their role for only a fraction of their serving lifespan in the church. My hope for them is they look back on youth leading and see it as a great time. A time where they both gave out and grew with Jesus.

This Big Ask also provides a platform for open faith conversations with leaders when we catch up. We are able to share our various lifestyle issues and wrestle together with what a "Jesus response" would be.

Most of all we want our leaders to know we are for them, Jesus is for them and we want to see them win in life and ministry. Their contribution is so much more than a task that needs doing. They are significant adults walking alongside their young people, shaping and moulding the next generation of Jesus-followers. They are role models and this is why looking after oneself and leading from a growing relationship with Jesus is so essential.

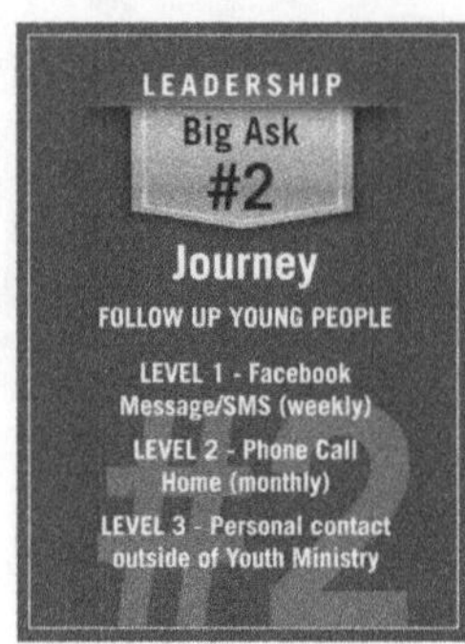

Big Ask #2: Follow Up Young People

At the heart of relational discipleship is life-on-life. Not 'life online' as my autocorrect just suggested: life-on-life! Think back to those who invested in you when you were young, both generally and in your spiritual formation. Was it your parents, a teacher, a pastor, an older sibling, or perhaps a volunteer youth leader? Did you learn from what they said or what they did? I guess, probably both.

I thank God for Scott Hawkins for first taking time to call me up and invite me to youth group. I thank God for Scott Berry who led me to Jesus and read the Bible with me, hung out with me and invited me into his world. I thank God for Jason Lippitt who walked with me through my senior years of high school. He encouraged me, challenged me and spent time shaping me. I thank God for my parents who raised me in the ways of the Kingdom of God. Who was it for you? Why not thank God for them right now and pray a blessing over their life, maybe even write them an encouraging note. It would make their day!

The Big Ask #2 is following up young people. This means caring for and loving a smaller group of young people and investing into their lives. This is vital if they are to grow in their journey of faith. The regular youth group experience is great and church is awesome, but if they don't have someone investing in a deeper way they can get lost. Christian parents are great, but not enough. The circle needs to be widened and this is where youth leaders can play such a vital role.

To use the language of relational currency, by following up we deposit relational currency and build trust into the lives of the young people in our care. At some point in the relationship we will withdraw relational currency as we challenge youth in their walk with God.

Ask youth leaders to be proactive in following up young people. Challenge them to put it in the diary and be intentional, as without this it is easy to fall away from regularly touching base and caring for young people. It helps to structure it so that every youth is in a life group and each life group leader has a group of approximately six to eight youth they care for.

To follow up, I recommend leaders use a three-level approach.[43]

- <u>Level 1</u> generates the least amount of relational currency and is the easiest to do. It consists of some kind of minimal contact (SMS, Facebook message, etc.) every week. Sometimes it's a group text regarding what's happening at youth group and sometimes it's an individual message.

- <u>Level 2</u> necessitates more of a deposit from the leader but it gives a return of greater relational currency. It's a phone call to each youth once a month. We ask leaders to call the home phone as they might also speak with one of the young person's parents, which is a win in terms of the family / church partnership.

- <u>Level 3</u> requires the greatest deposit of time from the leader but has the biggest relational impact. It's a personal visit / activity once a year with each youth in their group. This generally equates to approximately one personal contact a month for the leader. This is huge, as personal visits and shared activities are so catalytic in helping a young person feel connected to the leader and the youth ministry, and this belonging often correlates to spiritual growth.

[43] My thanks to Gavin Brown and Scott Morrison for their leadership and insights in helping me develop this work.

I love hearing stories of youth leaders surprising youth by watching their football matches or going to their musical theatre performances. I love it even more when parents tell me about it and how appreciative they are.

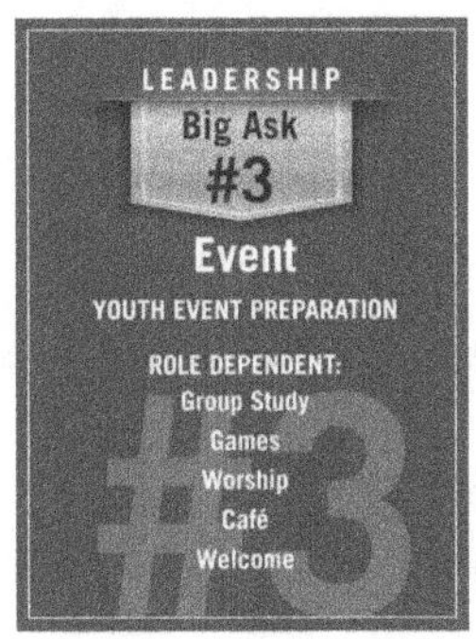

Big Ask #3: Prepare for Game Time

Big Asks #1 and #2 focus on the journey of faith. Big Asks #3 and #4 focus on the other major element of youth leading, the weekly youth event. We are all on a journey in life and faith, and an important aspect of this is to cluster together in bigger events to worship, be taught the word of God, build community and grow in God's plans for us.

Events for their own sake have a short-term impact and rarely bear lasting fruit. Events that focus on seeking God, reaching teenagers with the gospel, mobilising mission and deepening community are so important. Therefore, our Big Ask #3 is to ask every leader to prepare well for the regular youth event. This will look different each week for leaders as roles and responsibilities vary. Sometimes it will mean preparing games, other times a Bible study, food for supper, worship songs or the message.

When I was going through teachers' college I heard a saying that has stuck with me. "If you fail to prepare, then prepare to fail."[44] I have found this to be true in most aspects of life, and ministry is no exception. I have a huge desire to see young leaders win in their leadership and also for youth to maximise their engagement in youth. Therefore, we need to ask our leaders to be prepared and ready for game time on a youth night.

Over the years I have found that younger leaders have a heart to plan but can forget, or are still learning, the art of time management. This Big Ask is helpful in highlighting the need to prepare well and be ready to minister to the young people God has given them at this time and stage of their lives.

Big Ask #4: Deliver on Game Time

It's 5pm on youth night. The members of your leadership team are coming to the end of their day and beginning to change gears for the youth group event. All of them have had different experiences during the week. Some have had massive weeks at work. Some have studied hard.

44 Wendy Piltz, Physical Education lecturer at Uni SA.

Some are cruising through university, and some have attained new levels on whatever game they are mastering. It's important to recognise that they haven't lived and breathed youth ministry during the week like you and I have.

We have a very real responsibility to help our leaders change gears and transition into their role at youth group. This is an ongoing challenge for us as key leaders.

That is why our fourth and final Big Ask is to deliver on the youth group event. Throughout my years leading young people, Friday night was always when we met together to celebrate what God was up to in our midst, to experience genuine community and to have fun. It might look a bit different for you, but gathering together is still vitally important. It's the time we create an environment for young people to belong and grow in their faith journey. It's our game time. We need to be on and focused to make the most of the limited corporate time we have together. It's important that we nail it!

To help your team it's important to clearly communicate your expectations. In practical terms, Big Ask #4 may mean, for example, being punctual for the pre-event prayer and briefing; being fully present with both the leaders and the young people; having the attitude of a servant as we actively serve our youth; delivering on the assigned role (for example, life group study, corporate prayer, preaching, running games); taking initiative in creating an effective atmosphere; making youth group feel safe for all youth, and helping with the clean-up at the end of the night.

You might think that this is all a no-brainer but unless you ask a leader, especially a younger one, to invest in this way, how will they know what to do? In building an effective team, it is important to make it really clear what you are asking as it sets the right expectations and provides essential guidelines. I have learnt that you do need to ask and keep on asking, in order to build this culture of preparedness amongst your team.

I have found that being this concrete, sets leaders up for a win. It keeps them focused and lifts the whole tone of the leadership team, because everyone knows what they need to get done on a youth night and what they need to do before they leave.

Four Big Ask Questions

How do you encourage your volunteer leaders to grow in their relationship with Jesus?

How do you structure your ministry so that personal follow up of each youth can occur?

Do you celebrate when your team nails it?

Do the parents know that "follow-up" is a value of your youth ministry?

Think about your leadership team right now. Who is usually prepared? Who can you say well done to? Who might you need to have a loving chat with, to help them step up their preparation?

WE FOCUS ON WHAT WE MEASURE

What is your main focus as a Youth Pastor? Is it:

- Ensuring the building doesn't get trashed?

- Not upsetting the parents?

- Being innovative and reaching young people for Jesus?

- Partnering with parents in the discipleship of their young people?

- Serving in the local high schools?

- Which café you will have lunch at tomorrow? (Ok, maybe that's just me.)

It is important to think seriously about what you focus on, because whether or not you consciously know it, we all focus on what we measure.

The question is, what do you measure? What is important to you? This can be tricky because when we talk about measurements, outcomes or goals, we can become like a turtle and seek to hide away! But, it's an important question to consider.

A few years ago, I joined a church with a really healthy leadership team that was asking questions about what God wanted us to achieve. Put simply, what were the God Desired Outcomes (GDOs)[45] we most wanted God to grace us with and bring into our midst? Of course, not for our own sake but for the advancement of His Kingdom. The ongoing conversation really sharpened the team and caused us all to look and assess what we did and why we did it. It helped us to focus on the main game of seeing people accept Jesus as Lord and begin a meaningful discipleship pathway towards maturity.

[45] Pastor Dale Stephenson introduced me to the term GDOs. I had always measured outcomes but didn't have a concise way of expressing this.

If it's true (and I think it is) that we focus on what we measure, what would be some gold standard measurement indicators for a healthy youth ministry? Let me suggest a few:

- Young people making first time commitments and significant recommitments in accepting Jesus as Lord and Saviour.

- Young people being baptised.

- Young people participating in life groups.

- Young people serving both inside and outside the church.

- Young people sharing their faith in their world: school, family, sporting clubs, part time jobs, dance groups, etc.

Measuring factors such as these would certainly make for a dynamic and challenging youth program, full of opportunities for gospel responses, baptisms, stories of lives transformed, small group engagement, and service both in and outside the church. Now that's the sort of group I would like to be leading!

If you could measure anything in the life of your youth ministry, what would it be and why?

COMMUNICATION IS KEY

In Australia, most of us take some time off during our summer, which is at the end of the calendar year. This is especially so in youth ministry, when the year winds up and we are usually fairly tired. But, when we get back on deck there is always a lot to do to get the year up and running. Before you know it, youth group activities will be launched and it will be a sprint until Easter. If you are struggling with what to prioritise, here are my three communication tips for the start of a ministry year.

1. Communicate to Leaders

January is the time to touch base relationally with your leaders. It could be a phone call, sharing a coffee, or an encouragement card. It's the time to hear the stories of summer and just enjoy hanging out without the immediate pressure of a regular youth event or an urgent ministry agenda.

It is also the time to sit down with the team to renew your commitment for the year ahead, put key dates in their diaries (seriously, make time for this), plan for term one and finalise any larger ideas / campaigns / projects that need clarity and direction.

2. Communicate to Parents

Send an email to parents in January with the theme for the year, key dates for the family diary, opportunities to serve, new initiatives, a link to any relevant social media pages, and an invitation to any key dates for term one (such as a parent's vision dessert night). Try to keep it brief and in bullet point form but craft it in a relational way.

In addition, look out for parents in the foyer on Sundays throughout January and make a real point of sharing when youth goes back and some of the big ideas for the year ahead. Ongoing communication with parents is vital in building trust and January is the best time to start this.

3. Communicate to Youth

There is nothing worse than a young person being out of the loop. Youth group needs to be a place where young people belong and they should feel this. If you don't know what's happening, it's easy to feel disconnected. During mid to late January, post regularly on social media with what's coming up so that all youth are in the loop. Ramp it up as school gets closer and, in the week of youth group going back, go hard!

You can also ask your leaders to connect with all their youth to touch base about the year ahead. This is so important in building a culture of relational discipleship.

What are some ways you communicate at the beginning of the year?

RECRUITING THE RIGHT KIND OF LEADER

Recruiting Volunteer Leaders

How do you identify the kind of volunteer leader you want on your team or, better yet, the kind of leader God wants on His team?

When it comes to recruiting, I'm guided by Bill Hybels' 4 Cs: character, competency, chemistry, and culture.[46] I believe character trumps the other three. At the end of the day, character

[46] The 3 C's are described in Bill Hybels, *Axiom: Powerful Leadership Provers* (Grand Rapids, Michigan: Zondervan, 2008), 75-77. The 4th C was introduced by Bill Hybels at the 2010 Global Leadership Summit during Session 1 on August 5th, 2010.

wins no matter how good someone is at something (competency) or how much I like them (chemistry) or even if they would be a great fit and add much to the team and ministry (culture). As Jim Collins says, when it comes to recruiting it is important to get the right person on the bus and then find them the right seat. The *who* comes before the *what*. The right person has the right character.[47]

Of course, we recruit people to roles and to perform a function, so it's important to know what they are passionate about and where they see they would best fit. The process of helping the person find the right seat on the bus is important but, above all, the right person has to have a heart for Jesus.

Here is an outline of how I have a face-to-face meeting with a volunteer leader I am seeking to recruit.

1. Ask them to share their story of faith development. Listen for their salvation story and where grace fits in.

2. If they approached you, ask them, "Why youth / young adults?" Once they have finished, share your vision and heart for the ministry and the need to have leaders like them investing in the next generation.

[47] Jim Collins, Good to Great (London, UK: Random House, 2001), 41.

3. If you approached them, share your vision and heart for the ministry and the need to have leaders like them investing in the next generation.

4. Ask them to share about their leadership experiences.

5. Share your vision for relational discipleship: the importance of making disciples and life-on-life discipleship.

6. Ask them what age group they have a passion for. This helps with life group leader placement.

7. Share the Four Big Asks, your basic expectations and the leader's covenant.

8. If all is going well (that is, they have the necessary competency and there is chemistry between you both), ask them to pray, chat to their family and seek God, and set up a time to meet again in a week or so.

9. Pray to close.

10. Follow up in a week or so to confirm their involvement or not.

My prayer for you is that you recruit well and have a team full of leaders who love Jesus and are growing with Him (character), who are great at what they do (competency), have a heap of fun along the way (chemistry), and mesh together for the long haul (culture).

How do you recruit leaders? Is there a potential leader you can sit down with and have the above conversation? Is there an emerging leader you can invest in, so that you can multiply your leadership deposit and they can begin their journey of recruiting the right kind of leader? If yes, who?

Hiring the Right Staff

I have been involved in lots of selecting and recruiting for roles, both from the church side as an employer and from the candidate side as employee. We know that if the discernment process is done well at the beginning, then there is a greater chance of setting up the incoming employee for a big win. With that in mind I have collated two sets of ten questions. I have called them, "Smart interview questions and smart interviewee questions".[48]

Smart Interview Questions:

1. Tell us a little about yourself and your faith journey.

---

[48] See: Dr Ken Byrne, *7 Secrets for Hiring the Best People* (Victoria, Australia), 2006.

2. What three words best describe your personality? Can you tell us about a time when these qualities have really helped you to be successful at work?

3. Why is this role attractive to you and why did you apply?

4. In your opinion what are the core elements in building and growing a healthy [insert ministry here] team? What is your experience of doing this in the past?

5. Can you tell us the most significant risk you took in your last job? Why did you take this risk?

6. What would be the single most stressful experience you have faced at work? How did you overcome it?

7. We've all had a time where we have had to sort out a difference of opinion at work with someone else. Can you describe a time when you have dealt with something like this?

8. Working at [insert organisational name here] is very dynamic and team orientated. Can you share with us how you have had to be flexible and display a teachable heart in the past?

9. As a disciple of Christ, what does the rhythm of your own personal spiritual formation look like?

10. Any questions for us?

The goal of these questions is to see behind the curtain of the candidate's life. It is to determine their character, chemistry and competency. Look for vulnerability, honesty and teach-ability, not just whether they can do the job. It is wise to put these questions into a table format and give a copy to each of the search team so that they can make notes and objectively compare candidates.

Smart Interviewee Questions:

1. Why did the last person leave? How long were they in the role?

2. How would you describe the health of [insert organisational name here]?

3. When you think about [insert organisational name here], what words come to mind? How would the unseen leaders in [insert organisational name here] answer this question?

4. How does the Senior Pastor lead? What leadership style would you say they have?

5. How is a sense of team fostered at [insert organisational name here]?

6. What are the expectations around this role? (Ask the search team, ask the Senior Pastor, ask the Board and look for alignment or lack of.)

7. Who does this role report to? What does the performance review cycle look like?

8. Any questions around theology to determine theological alignment.

9. How will the church integrate and care for my family?

10. What will [insert organisational name here] look like in five year's time? How will [insert organisational name here] cope with change?

The goal of these questions is to seek out the true culture of the church by asking leading questions. It is vital the potential employee knows the health of the church, leadership style of their leader, expectations of the role and where the organisation sees its future. The potential employee needs to seek God's wisdom on alignment, potential conflict and areas of opportunity into the future.

Are there any other questions you think need asking?

Building Relational Currency in Our Volunteer Teams

The challenge for any volunteer-based team is to keep volunteers fully engaged for the entire duration of the program. In my experience, when it comes to individual events or even weekend or week long camps, this isn't too much of a challenge. The odd motivational pep talk and inspiring leadership proverb, along with the promise that this will soon be over and there is plenty of sweet rest to come, can get most people across the line! Inspiring leaders to back up week after week, term after term, and (we pray) year after year, is a whole different challenge. Great speeches are not enough. Our leaders need more motivation to keep coming back and giving their all no matter what challenges they face.

In our working lives we generally receive a financial incentive to keep us coming each day, but what do our volunteer leaders receive as payment? A good feeling? A rewarding experience? The satisfaction of knowing they are serving an incredible, loving God? Those are great when things are going well but I've found that when ministry gets tough, our volunteer leaders need more from us than just a reminder of how they could or should be feeling. They need leaders who can offer them a return greater than what they could receive in their part time job, study or sporting lives; a return that answers some of their deepest needs. We may not be able to pay them financially, but in ministry we can so easily become experts in creating relational currency.

Our leaders need to know first and foremost that they are loved and appreciated by us for who they are. Not what they can offer us, not their skills and abilities, but for the person God made them to be.

Secondly, they need to sense that we value their faith highly and will do whatever it takes to ensure that they are strong men and women of faith by the time they leave our ministry.

Thirdly, and only after the first two points are 100% understood by our leaders, do we focus on what they bring to our ministry. A person who senses that this is how they are valued by their leader will come back again and again, regardless of the challenges, as they experience some of their deepest needs being met. We all need to know we are deeply valued for who we are. No matter what we do, we want to be accepted and to feel like we can truly be ourselves.

We all feel abundantly blessed when someone takes the time to invest into our faith. This payment is a greater reward than any financial payment we receive, which is why we are more than happy to pay hard cash for conferences, books and other resources that will grow our faith. **When our leaders know that they are highly valued and are 'paid' week in and week out with a growing faith, more often than not they will want to use their gifts to serve our ministries in the face of whatever challenges are thrown their way.**

TEAM RETREATS

Each year I plan for a team retreat. Sometimes it is a day, sometimes it is a weekend; it all depends on what we need to get done and the availability of the team. Last year we went away for the weekend. We arrived at 8pm on the Friday night to a beautiful beach house (heavily discounted by one of our congregational members) and left again at 2pm on the Sunday. It was a whirlwind of fun, worship, creative problem solving, food and time to seek after God's heart for the future plans of the ministry. If you are not into retreats or have never really thought they were valuable, I'd like to challenge you on this.

Why?

Retreats are important because they enable:

Quality time as a team

Quality time is essential for building relationship and trust. This simply cannot happen over a few hours on a Friday night when you are focused on the youth. "Quality time = quantity time"[49] and a retreat enables a significant amount of time together as a team. When a team spends quality and quantity time together, the outcome is almost always that they align and sharpen one another for the mission of making disciples.

Group spiritual formation

Whenever I run a team retreat I factor in some extended spiritual formation time, such as group Bible learning (for example, Lectio Divina), leadership teaching, silent prayer retreat time, extended worship, group sharing and prayer. This is important because it prioritises our intimacy with Jesus, and refocuses and renews the team.

Time to have fun and connect

The team that has fun together stays together! As a team, you need to make time to laugh and have fun, drop your guard, connect

[49] Adam Low, Youth Pastor at Clovercrest Baptist church, 2006.

and discover who the competitive team members are. You don't have to spend heaps of money. Games are a great source of fun. They are even better when you make your own rules and create fun memories that way.

A time of intense productivity

Like an intensive subject at college that counts for a whole semester of normal classes, a team retreat is a great way to get serious amounts of work done in one hit. The God-outcomes are huge and the pay off in terms of productivity is invaluable.

Who?

Once you are convinced that a retreat is the way to go, the next question is, "Who should I invite?" Understanding that volunteers give so much already and that everyone's time is so valuable, who are the best people to bring along?

It is important that you include your key decision makers; your core team. My core team consists of those with leadership responsibility over different areas or departments of the ministry.

Depending on the size of your leadership team, it will probably be a mix of staff and volunteers, or all volunteers. If your team is smaller, make sure you have the people that you trust and know will add to the conversation. Having the right mix of people is essential.

When you are choosing your key players, consider not only those who are leading with you now, but also those who are coming through the ranks and will be leaders in the future. Who are your future guns that would value the experience of coming away with the core team?

When?

I have been involved in different teams over the years and we have retreated at various times for a range of reasons. We have had summer retreats in January or early February to set the year up. I've been away in May to see how the year has started and ask questions about whether we are on the right track. The timing depends on your focus and the desired outcome for the retreat.

With all of this in mind, I am going to give you my preferred option. My Vision Team's main aim is to review the year and look ahead into the next year. Therefore, my preferred time to retreat is… drumroll please... early October.

In Australia, early October is the start of term four (our final school term for the year). We are in the last quarter of activity for the year and enough has happened to warrant a solid and comprehensive review. But, it is also close enough to the next year that we can dream, pray and brainstorm with purpose so that firm plans and initiatives can be discussed. Put simply, it's the perfect time to look back and also look forward.

Early October works for other reasons as well. It is just before the university exam period. This will affect leaders who are studying, and in my context this is a large percentage. Moreover, our budget cycle is well under way for the following year, so we can be on the front foot to plan for new initiatives in the coming year.

From a leadership perspective, it also gives a big push for our key leaders to finish the year well and envision plans for the following year, which is a positive momentum builder. Term four can historically be a time of winding down but, by having a retreat in October, it helps you stay motivated into the Christmas period.

What?

Below is a run sheet from a recent team retreat. I planned for a balance of fun and work: lots of time for games and building relationships as well as looking to outcomes. I partnered people together to provide for meals. If you can, pay for the Saturday night meal. This is a great way of honouring your volunteers for the time they invest. Perhaps ask your Senior Pastor for some funds for this. I hope they would be keen to invest into the next generation of leaders!

Friday night (optional)	
Arrive after work	Provide own meal on the way down
	Hang out / games
Saturday	
8:30 am	Breakfast
9:00 am	Prayer retreat • Devotion • Group sharing and prayer
9:30 am	Silent time • Read through a passage of scripture • Pray, listen, be still
11:00 am	Reflection back and pray for each other • What was God saying? / What do I / we need to do about it?
12 noon	Lunch

12:30 pm	Group Activity – Fun and team building
4:00 pm	Review current year • Progress on yearly goals • Other celebrations • Challenges / issues • Opportunities / where the ministry is heading • Budget review • General vibe from each team member • Stopping any initiatives that are ineffective – mission drift?
7:30 pm	Dinner
9:00 pm	Games
Sunday	
8:30 am	Breakfast
9:00 am	Worship / prayer / devotion

10:00 am	Next year's big rocks
	
	• Budget forecast
	• Broad term themes
	    > terms 1 - 4 (butcher's paper)
	• Focus for blessing volunteers
	    > ($5 how would we spend it on them?)
	• Strategy to achieve goals
	    > 'Marry the mission, date the method'
	    > New initiatives

12 noon	Working lunch
1:00 pm	Clean up
2:00 pm	Leave by 2:00 pm

Write a list of who you need to take on a retreat and what you need to achieve to get the maximum result.

LAST QUARTER CONVERSATIONS

I have learned that there are usually two main reasons why a volunteer leader asks to have a meeting with me during the last quarter of a calendar year, that is, September to December. As the year comes to an end, most people are beginning to think about the new year and my calendar begins to fill up with leaders who I generally don't have the privilege of spending a lot of one-on-one time with. These leaders are usually high quality, high capacity, up and coming or seasoned leaders. The kind of leaders that when I see their name, I think, "No, don't you be going anywhere!"

After the initial chat and catching up, the conversation usually goes one of two ways.

1. I am finishing up.
2. I want more responsibility.

To be honest, the "I am finishing up" conversation is the one I have more often at this time of year. Before I go off to a corner and cry myself to sleep, I stop and think: how can we get a win-win out of this? There are some leaders we are happy to see go as they have lost the drive and passion, but there are others that make me think, "I don't want to lose you. How could we reshape your role to better fit with your changing passions?"

I often anticipate this conversation and consider in advance of the meeting:

- What are their passions and skill set?

- Is it time for them to go or is there another conversation to be had?

- How could we reshape or value-add with them in another role?

- Will this compromise the purpose of our mission of making disciples?

Sometimes you can make it work and other times you just need to say goodbye. In any case, it's worth taking five minutes to do a quick assessment so that when the conversations come, you are ready and armed with positive ideas for how the ministry can move forward!

Consider your ministry team. What is the chemistry like? What role does each member have? What movements do you anticipate in the next year? Who might be moving on and who is needing to step up?

Helping Leaders Say Goodbye

Recently I had one of my young gun leaders ask for a meeting. I knew she had been battling with some personal stuff – nothing sinister – but front and centre of her processing was what church to attend and where to serve.

As I prepared for the meeting and prayed for her, I braced myself for what I thought was coming.

When she arrived, the news I was dreading came out. She told me she was leaving. She loved our church, but was following God's call and moving to another church. As she shared, and I felt a little part of my heart break (she is awesome and I know how much her life group girls loved her), I knew my reaction was important. This is what I did next.

1. I told her I was very sad to see her go and we would miss her.

2. I affirmed that I was proud of the way she had processed this move so maturely.

3. I asked her to say goodbye to her life group girls well.

4. I wished her all the best for the future and prayed a blessing over her life.

I was trying to be affirming yet honest, whilst also helping her to have a concrete way to finish well. In a way, I was finishing well with my young leader so that she could finish well with her girls. As a young emerging leader, I wanted her to feel she could go on and lead well from the experience she had under my leadership.

I knew that her leaving would shock some of her girls, so we decided that she would:

- Write a card to the fringe girls.

- Make a phone call to the regular girls.

- Personally catch up with the girls with whom she was especially close, who would take her leaving the hardest.

Each goodbye has a relational edge and I asked her to say goodbye in a way that would set her replacement leader up for a win. This is so important in ministry of any kind, but especially youth ministry, where we are constantly working with youth who are still maturing.

It's very true that people don't notice how you start, but they do notice how you finish. So as leaders let's display dignity and grace and help our volunteer leaders finish well.

How do you help your leaders say their goodbyes?

IT'S VERY TRUE THAT PEOPLE DON'T NOTICE HOW YOU START, BUT THEY DO NOTICE HOW YOU FINISH.

If relationship is the glue of ministry, then effective leadership is the applicator. While it is possible to compel people through a role or title; relationship applies the appropriate amount of encouragement and challenge with genuine care. This type of relational leadership over time makes for a strong bond as we grant someone access to the trials and triumphs of our own experience and trust that integrity ultimately shines through.

Leadership is about drawing the best out of others and creating opportunities for that to find expression. Often, it's about seeing more in a person than they initially see in themselves. One of my proudest moments as a leader was seeing Rachel, one of my youth leaders, preach at a Crossway evening service. My mission to get her onto this highly exclusive platform, where she delivered an incredible message with true authority, was *five years* in the making (and many more from God's perspective!). I'm convinced a leader's greatest moments are those out of the spotlight as, perhaps for a moment, we get a glimpse at what God sees in someone else.

As I reflect on what it means to lead others through change and growth, I'm reminded of a deeply profound question, first introduced to me by Margaret Spicer, that I now always include when recruiting potential leaders: *"How do you think God wants to grow you through this ministry?"* It's sobering to consider how rarely this question is asked, often found hidden under the piles of questions as to how one will contribute to a ministry, rather than flourish through it. As Mike has stressed all the way through this section, while providing a consistent leadership contribution to a team is valiant, it can actually become the adversary of true influence being multiplied in and through one's ministry. After all, first and foremost, as leaders we reproduce who we are.

At the risk of pride, first remind yourself that all you have is a gift from God, then take a moment to consider – **what parts of me have I seen multiplied in those around me?**

Characteristic or Competency	Who do I see it in?
1.	
2.	

When we lead others well, and witness the fruit of our influence, we not only articulate a relational approach to discipleship, we live it out.

This section began with the simple statement that producing effective, gospel-orientated leaders must be a priority. Those two descriptive words will never cease to challenge me about my own leadership and the teams I form around a shared vision. Effective, does it actually work? Gospel-orientated, does it ultimately matter? That, in and of itself is not a bad diagnostic tool as we consider how this essential glue of relationship is applied!

MAKE THE GLUE STICK

1. Which of the **Four Big Asks** do my leaders need greater accountability in right now?

- [ ] **Lead From Your Growing Relationship with Jesus**
- [ ] **Follow Up Young People**
- [ ] **Prepare for Game Time**
- [ ] **Deliver on Game Time**

2. In which of my leader(s) am I specifically endeavouring to **multiply myself?**

(Name) ________________________________

3. As I consider the **time, resources,** and **energy** used in the ministry that I am involved with, where would it fit on this continuum?

High Development Focus   **High Delivery Focus**

← - →

4. Are there any changes I need to make to balance this? Who do I need to speak to?

- my supervisor

- my team

- an external mentor

- my Lead Pastor

(Send them a text message right now.)

To strategically and sacrificially lead others is both a personal and corporate challenge, yet this type of investment becomes the primary catalyst for a ministry to be both healthy and sought-after by volunteers. Leaders will stick, and become your greatest legacy.

THINK	**ACT**
Do our leaders leave well, or is there something more I can to do to ensure these steps are celebrated?	Consider your context and articulate what the "Big Asks" would be for your leaders.
How can I listen better? What could regular and effective feedback loops look like?	Prioritise and set a date for a team retreat.
How can I communicate better to our youth, parents, and my own team?	Write up a process or flow-chart for helping orientate new leaders.

YOUTH MINISTRY ESSENTIALS

Once the big rocks are in place and we have begun to develop a leadership culture, we are ready to explore youth ministry essentials. People will always be more important than programs, however there comes a time to explore the strategic aspects of youth ministry.

I have been involved in youth ministry since being a young person myself. I remember leading my first event as a student leader in year eleven. It was a beach night! Since 2005 I have lived and breathed youth ministry in a paid capacity and have sought to be a learner and to be committed to best practice.

Over the years, I have been blessed with working alongside some of the most talented paid and volunteer teams around. This has sharpened my thinking and practice.

In this section I have zoomed out to 40,000 feet above sea level to describe the bigger picture and essential practices cultivated by an effective youth ministry. These are:

1: DEVELOPING A DISCIPLESHIP CULTURE

2: PARTNERING WITH PARENTS

3: HEALTHY LIFE GROUPS

4: A FOCUS ON TRANSITIONS

5: LEVERAGING PEAK EXPERIENCES

6: BIG EVENTS

DEVELOPING A DISCIPLESHIP CULTURE

The goal of any healthy and thriving youth ministry is to effectively reach and grow disciples of Jesus, who in turn multiply their lives into others. The image of yeast going through dough to make the bread rise is one Jesus used as a picture of the Kingdom of God.[50] As faith develops in a young person, it is natural for it to grow into all the relational areas of their lives. Author and speaker Stephen Aterburn describes it like this, "As faith matures, it integrates."[51]

For faith to integrate into the life of a young person, we need to ensure we have a holistic approach to discipleship. Discipleship isn't purely an intellectual pursuit (head), or an emotional response to God (heart), or simply living out our faith (hands). It is actually all three of these things, all at the same time: Head, Heart, and Hands.[52]

[50] Matthew 13: 33

[51] Steve Arterburn, Lifewell Conference Australia, August 2011.

[52] Head, Heart, Hands is a well-known holistic discipleship pathway process, but I first heard it from Andrew Palmer in 2010 when he was the NSW/ ACT State Youth Director for the Baptist Churches.

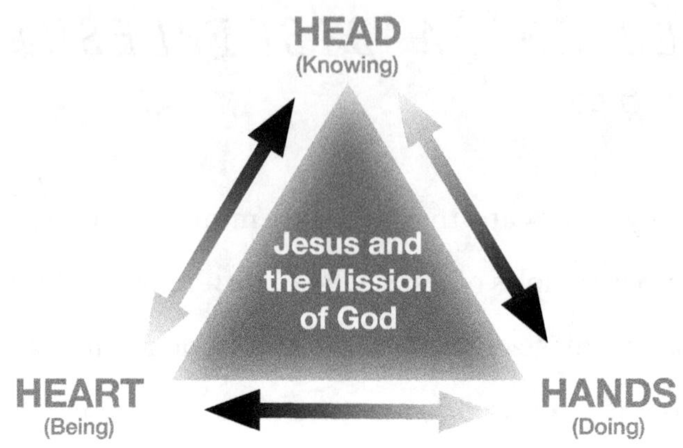

The triangle above visually represents this holistic, integrated discipleship model. Let's take a look at each aspect.

- Head: It's important to know Christ and to have an understanding of His life and power. We need to spend time studying the Word and to have a real and growing intellectual grasp of the truth.

- Heart: It's vital to be in God's presence and grow with a soft heart towards total obedience to Him and His ways. Corporate prayer and worship, accountability in community and being connected into God's family are essential in a growing faith.

- Hands: It's not enough merely to think it or have a heart for it, faith needs to be lived out through daily obedience. The actions of our hands and feet demonstrate what we really believe. We reflect Jesus to our friends, family and the world when they see us living for truth and justice, compassion and love.

It's been my goal and desire to grow healthy, well rounded disciples that know Christ, have a heart of obedience to His ways, and live out Kingdom values in their everyday lives.

How does your youth ministry reflect the Head, Heart, Hands integrated approach to discipleship?

Are all three areas in balance, or do you have an over-emphasis in one direction that needs correcting?

Behaviour That Demonstrates a Discipleship Culture

Culture is a funny thing. Lots of leaders talk about it and want to develop it, but not many really know how. One thing I have learnt is that if you want to grow a culture, you need to name it and set some preferred outcomes around it so you know what you are aiming for.

When I was leading the youth team at Crossway, we quite intentionally sought to develop a culture of integrated discipleship. We named some behaviours we wanted to cultivate in our young people. If we saw that behaviour grow, we knew we were growing in culture. If we didn't, well then we had more work to do.

We measured the growth of this behaviour through life groups, based on the observations of group leaders. Because the group sizes were small, people were in relationship and knew each other, so qualitative measurements were more likely to be accurate.

The indicators we used to signify the growth of a healthy discipleship culture in our youth community were:

- Asking better questions.
- Being on mission in their school and / or local community.

- Promoting issues of justice.

- Actively caring for each other.

- Having an openness to new people in their lives.

- Multiplying their life group as more people joined.

The behaviours we measured are articulated in the following graphic.[53]

A BETTER QUESTION

This culture is one of discovery, employing the art of questioning as a central means of discipleship and growth within Life Groups. Seeking wisdom and guidance outside their own experience, youth are not afraid to ask questions in the confidence that they will not be judged. Lead by the Spirit into all truth, freedom is found as youth strive to discover, engage, and wrestle with the reality of a loving yet mysterious God through his Word.

COMMISSIONING THE NOW

This culture promotes the truth that a youth's current context, season, and relational circles are their mission field. When we Commission the Now, youth are prayerfully empowered and mobilized for Kingdom work, while as Life Groups we are intentional to seek and celebrate the stories that arise out of an extraordinary God working through ordinary circumstances. The eyes of our youth are opened to the missional opportunities that exist within their everyday lives.

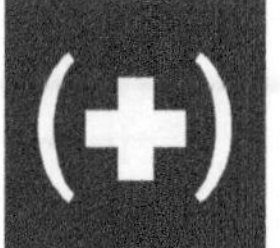

HANDS THAT HEAL

This is a culture of justice, with Life Groups intentionally reaching out in acts of loving service to others, both global and local. Youth regularly encounter and are impacted by the brokenness that they see, and respond with a deep conviction to act on behalf of those oppressed. This culture petitions for active service outside of the ministry – bringing light into darkness, and doing it all in God's name, partnering with him in his mission of restoration.

INTERNAL PASTORAL INITIATIVE (IPI)

This is a culture where youth are empowered to intentionally invest in and care for the lives of their peers, taking pastoral initiative that leads to healing, growth and understanding. IPI moves away from the traditional vertical model of follow-up, and rather promotes horizontal engagement where ultimately every young person can feel comfortable both being cared for, and caring for another within their Life Groups.

AN OPEN CIRCLE

This is a culture in which each Life Group exists in a constant state of invitation, both encouraging and anticipating that new members will join in the journey of Christian community with them. An Open Circle makes the first move toward those youth on the fringe, authentically seeking relationship and connection despite diversity valuing both the person and their unique contribution to the Life Groups.

FREE2MULTIPLY

This culture both deliberately works toward then celebrates the time when a Life Group must multiply as a refining and purposeful movement that will lead to future growth. With a perspective of God's greater mission, seasons of small community are understood and appreciated as a valuable yet temporary, with exciting new horizons and stories to encounter.

[53] Gavin Brown, Crossway 2011

How do your life groups capture Kingdom health and growth?

How do you know your young people are growing in an integrated approach to discipleship?

PARTNERING WITH PARENTS

If you have got this far in the book, then I'm sure you agree with an earlier statement I quoted from David Kinnaman that, "Disciples are handmade and not mass produced."[54] Having committed, genuine and authentic leaders walking alongside our young people is so important.

But having competent, Jesus-loving leaders is not enough. It is actually the wrong place to start in the discipleship process. **Home is where discipleship begins because parents are the primary**

<hr>

[54] David Kinnaman, 13.

disciplers.[55] There is no perfect family and no perfect church, but we need to work together and not in competition with each other.[56]

The current research confirms what we already know. The Fuller Youth Institute tells us that parents are the biggest role models in a young person's life and remain the number one influence in youth faith development. Their research suggests that kids adopt the depth of faith of their parents.[57] Faith formation cannot be outsourced, that is a flawed ministry paradigm. To be effective, what we do at youth must somehow push into the other six and a half days of the week. And to achieve this, we need to partner with parents!

The *Think Orange* team have identified that we have approximately forty structured hours with a young person in church each year, compared to three thousand annual unstructured hours that they

[55] Reggie Joiner, *Think Orange: Imagine the Impact when Church and Family* Collide (Colorado Springs, USA: David Cook Distribution, 2009), 84.

[56] Reggie Joiner, 95-96 and Reggie Joiner and Carey Nieuwhof, *Parenting Beyond Your Capacity: Connect Your Family to a Wider Community* (Colorado Springs, USA: David Cook Distribution, 2011), 44.

[57] Dr Kara Powell, Brad Griffin and Dr Cheryl Crawford, *Sticky Faith: Youth Worker Ed* (Grand Rapids, Michigan: Zondervan, 2011), 116-117.

have with their families.[58] The Founder of *Think Orange*, Reggie Joiner, says "Two combined influences are more effective than two separate influences". This is at the heart of *Think Orange* as it aims to combine and integrate the red from home and the yellow from church to make orange![59]

The *40 Developmental Assets* team has researched the building blocks for healthy development and four of the assets explicitly mention family and parents.[60] They are: family support, positive family communication, family boundaries, and adult role models. As young people are exposed to these things they develop health in themselves.

If family is such a vital part of a young person's life, then why, when I look at best practice youth ministry around our nation, don't I hear more about partnering with parents? Is this thinking on your radar?

[58] Reggie Joiner, 87-88.

[59] Reggie Joiner, 16 and 95.

[60] http://www.search-institute.org/content/40-developmental-assets-adolescents-ages-12-18 accessed 14/04/2017

4 Stages of Parental Engagement

When we bring parents into the ministry conversation it doesn't take long to realise that they have varying levels of commitment to the discipleship process of their young person. A really helpful tool from the *Think Orange* team is the 'Stages of Parental Engagement.'[61] The tool identifies four stages that should be read in a linear way from non-engaged to fully engaged. Let's take a look at the stages.

1. <u>Aware</u>: Want to be better parents, are concerned about their kids growing and improving as people but are generally not connected into church life.

2. <u>Involved</u>: Basic, entry level relationship with the church, even if it's just bringing their kids to church. They take some responsibility for growing the spiritual dynamic of their kids' lives.

3. <u>Engaged</u>: Committed to partnering with the church, take responsibility for their own faith and their young person's faith development.

4. <u>Invested</u>: Proactively devote time and energy to partnering with the church.

[61] Reggie Joiner, 164.

The Youth Pastor's role is to educate parents and try to move them along the stages as we journey through relationship and time. Typically, the majority of parents tend to be in the aware and involved stages, with a much smaller percentage in the engaged and invested stages. I'm encouraged by this tool as it names this reality and gives concrete options for moving forward and building engagement.

Where are your parents in the stages of engagement? Map your parents under the four stages and think about which parents you can be moving from one stage to the next.

Promoting Parent Discipleship – Building Awareness

This is vital in partnering with parents. I have found it provides practical opportunities for parents to move from the aware stage to the involved stage of parental engagement. Over the years, I have been involved in teams that do two things to build awareness.

1. Tell parents they are the primary disciplers

Parent nights offer an ideal opportunity to do this. My recommendation is to schedule one at the beginning of the year to outline the vision and plan for the year and seek response and partnering strategies from parents. Follow up with regular emails containing information about the youth ministry, and articles or websites to build awareness and empower parents to be the primary disciplers. This can be articulated at the year six graduation night for new youth and parents who are joining the youth community, when it's made really clear that parents are their children's primary disciplers.

2. Let parents know we are partnering them

The leadership axiom that "language matters"[62] is so true. Language repeated over time precedes the culture that will be formed in an organisation. It is really helpful to speak a consistent language of partnership across your generational teams. Over time, this will turn into culture as children, youth and young adults and their parents, consistently hear the same message and values spoken into their lives.

---

[62] Bill Hybels, *Axiom: Powerful Leadership Proverbs* (Grand Rapids, Michigan: Zondervan, 2008), 17-20.

From my experience, increased ongoing communication and relationship building is vital to building awareness. It was a running joke that I was Youth Pastor to the parents. I'd say hi to them in the car park, email regularly, have an open door for chats, ask for feedback and generally try to be as approachable as possible. This coincided with our pastoral issues going through the roof! I'm convinced that we didn't suddenly have a particularly higher rate of incidents going on in the lives of our youth, but due to increased communication and relationship with families, and an understanding of our partnering with them, we were invited to help and assist more often.

How can you build more awareness in your parents' world that they are their children's primary disciplers?

Promoting Parent Discipleship – Creating Opportunity

On summer days when I reach for my sunglasses, it is so good not to have to squint and struggle with the extra glare from the sun.

If I know anything about youth ministry, it's that Youth Pastors don't need to do more work. What I have been proposing about partnering with parents will mean putting on your sunnies and getting a clearer focus on what lies ahead for you in your ministry context. How can you put a parent lens on those sunnies and have a fresh look over your youth ministry, to see where you can be making some adjustments and sharpening things for a bigger win in making disciples?

In partnering with parents, after building awareness comes creating opportunity. From my experience, creating opportunity is really for parents in the engaged and invested stages. This is about creating opportunity for them to take the lead in the discipleship pathway for their young person and to really step up and own it. Once they start doing this for their own family, it is a real joy when you start seeing them do this in the lives of other families as well.

I see the Youth Pastor's role as creating lots of different opportunities for parents to engage in this discipleship process.

Here are just some of the ways we can do this:

- Table talk material: Provide regular family devotionals to facilitate faith conversations around the kitchen table during the evening meal time.

- Youth camp news: Send home nightly emails with highlights and photos to bring the camp experience into the home. On the last day of camp, meet with parents half an hour before the bus arrives and speak to them about camp (highlights, challenges, etc.) and share with them a couple of conversation starter tips to help them take the lead as the primary disciplers. I've experienced huge wins from this.

- Parent involvement on youth nights: Parents of the younger crew (years seven to nine) are particularly willing to get involved.

- Parenting teenagers course: Run by parents for parents. This is really letting invested parents loose. They now are serving and shaping the culture of what the parent partnership actually looks like.

- <u>Pastoral care for volunteer leaders</u>: For example, older parents who mentor younger leaders. This inter-generational connection can be so valuable to the young leaders and helps some of the older people find a place to serve once their children have grown up. Leadership development cascades down the generations as we promote partnering with parents.

Look at your own ministry and context and answer the question, what am I already doing? Then put a parent lens on it and see what changes you can make to begin / advance your partnership with parents and families. The aim is not to work harder but smarter. To put on your sunglasses to stop the glare and distraction, and get some new and renewed focus. You can't do everything, but you can do something. What is your something?

How can you create more opportunities for parents to step up as the primary disciples?

The Importance of Connecting with Parents

As I have mentioned on previous pages, having a Parent Night is an important way to connect with parents. Make sure there are lots of delicious sweets, the coffee machine is primed and you are ready to chat with parents about their most precious possession, their young person. I recommend doing this at the start of the year for many reasons. Here are my top four:

1. To reconnect after summer holidays

People don't always just naturally connect and the bigger the church, the harder we need to work to create connection points. Parent nights are a great connection place. Therefore, the first hour of the night is simply eating nice food, having coffee and allowing space for parents to reconnect and maybe connect for the first time.

2. To connect the new year seven parents in with the committed core who come out to evening sessions

New year seven parents might not know the other parents of youth, especially if your church runs multiple services on a Sunday. A parent night allows a safe environment for parents to meet and share details with other parents they don't know.

3. To explore new initiatives and share broader goals for the year

The parent night is a place to share vision and goals for the year. It's good to be open and explicit around this. Parents need to know we have outcomes we are working towards and see opportunities for them to participate and own the ministry. It also helps them be more informed in how they pray for the ministry. Share key dates and new initiatives, ask them questions and ask for their assistance and support. You can ask for their feedback and wisdom on how to deliver on some of your goals as well.

4. To remind us all what is more important in the discipleship process

We've seen that parents are the primary disciplers. This is not a new idea but, as we know, vision can dissipate and we need to keep coming back to it. Spend some time during your parent night exploring this practically and having a short teaching and reflection time to make it personal. I've found that this works well towards the end of the night, as it gets the parents working and is a deep and personal way to close your time together.

How do you connect with your parent community?

HEALTHY LIFE GROUPS

Big = Small

I had the privilege of sitting with and chatting to a legend of the faith here in Australia. I asked him what I needed to know about church leadership now and into the future. He said to me, "Mike, as church gets bigger, it has to get smaller."[63]

This was a profound statement as we live in an age where we can be connected to everyone, without necessarily really knowing anyone. Our role as pastors and leaders is to create rich and meaningful connection points, and one way to do this is through life groups.

Life groups are essential in youth ministry. We have to move from the paradigm of the crowd to focus on the community and,

---

[63] Peter Corney, whose teaching has shaped my ministry thinking over the last 10 years.

even more, on the core.[64] Life groups facilitate knowing people and being known, which is essential in a relational discipleship approach.

I love the *Think Orange* strategy of not having rows but creating circles from a young age.[65] For example, my daughter was led in kid's church by a beautiful young adult. That young adult was in a life group and was being mentored by a wonderful lady in the church. Having significant adults that walk alongside younger people is essential.

As Paul said to the Corinthians, "Imitate me as I imitate Christ."[66] We all imitate someone or something – it's how we are wired – so let's point people to Jesus. The best way to do this is in smaller life groups where love and accountability are naturally fostered.

Mission Through Smaller Groups

Praying and being on mission are essentials of being a disciple of Jesus Christ. An excellent way to cultivate these behaviours is in

[64] Rick Warren, *Purpose Driven Church: Growth without Compromising Your Message and Mission* (Grand Rapids, Michigan: Zondervan, 1995), 309-393.

[65] Reggie Joiner, Kristen Ivy and Elle Campbell, *Creating a Lead Small Culture: Making Your Church a Place Where kids belong* (Cumming, USA: Orange, 2014), 170-184.

[66] 1 Corinthians 11: 1

smaller groups, including life groups. In the past I have walked alongside smaller groups of young people seeking to grow and develop. We went prayer walking; served the homeless at soup kitchens; performed backyard blitzes for local community people; studied the Word together; shared our faith with those in our relational worlds, and held one another accountable.

One of my favourite experiences of this was leading small groups of young people to our local soup kitchen where we served the most disadvantaged of our community. It was such a privilege to drive into the city and pray for our time together. Then, when we were at the soup kitchen, breaking off into smaller groups to do different jobs. Watching young people engage with people different to them and being the hands and feet of Jesus was so inspiring.

One resource that I have found to be really helpful in cultivating mission in a life group context is the 3DM approach to discipleship, leadership and mission. This encourages life groups to have a rhythm of UP, IN and OUT.[67] The following diagram describes this some more.

[67] Mike Breen, *Building a Discipling Culture: How to release a missional movement by discipling people like Jesus did* (Pawleys Island, USA: 3DM, 2011), 67-70.

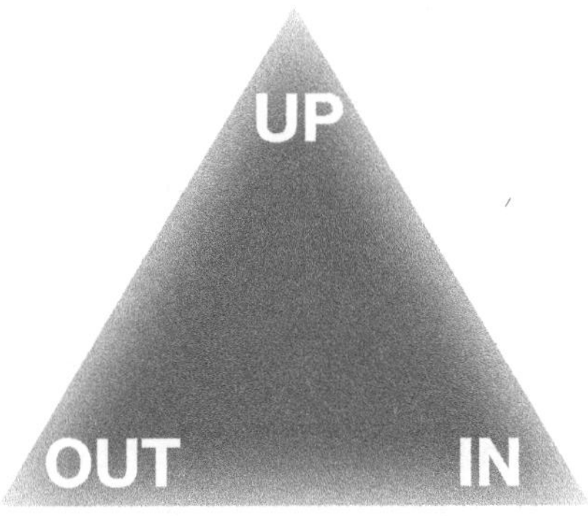

UP – Spend time praying with one another

IN – Spend time in community caring for one other

OUT – Spend time on mission with one another

Effective youth ministries use smaller groups as a vehicle for advancing the Kingdom of God. In smaller groups, bonds can be created, faith risks can take place, and loving accountability can occur.

Do you have life groups as an essential part of your youth ministry? Why or why not? How does your youth ministry utilise smaller groups for mission?

A FOCUS ON TRANSITIONS

Five Reasons Why Transitions Need to be on Your Radar

Do you ever find yourself wondering where past youth who were once in your care are now? Have they continued in faith or dropped out of church life? It's sad to ponder, but we would all have people come to mind that have disengaged from the church.

It goes without saying that we all want to see a decrease in the drop off rates from children to youth and from youth to young adults. One way we can address this is by focusing on our most vulnerable transition points: from year six into year seven, when youth come from kids' ministry into youth ministry, and from year twelve into university or the workplace, where youth go from youth ministry into young adults' ministry.

Let me give you five reasons why a focus on transitions is an essential of youth ministry.

1. <u>It directly targets the faith and community drop off that we are seeing across our nation</u>

There is a scary reality that we must face: young people are walking away from faith communities at an alarming rate. We need to act yesterday. That's right, we are already too late. Urgency is needed. People's lives are literally at risk, so we need to act on this right away.

2. It builds greater team unity amongst your next generation team (birth to 30 years)

Unity in church teams is so important. When we are dis-unified we drop the ball on the main game of making disciples and become distracted by things of lesser importance. If you have a common goal that everyone supports, such as facilitating successful transitions, this will naturally bring unity to your operations.

3. It builds greater ministry alignment amongst your next generation team

Where there is unity, alignment comes and ministry outcomes increase. From my experience, when the next generation team (children and families, youth and young adults) begin to have relational alignment and ministry alignment, an increase in missional outcomes usually follows. It's also a lot of fun to work towards common outcomes across departments in a team environment!

4. <u>It is a proactive approach that sets the youth and the ministry up for a win</u>

We need to be proactive in our approach to youth ministry. By widening our ministry lens to take in the person from birth to around thirty (far beyond our specific Youth Pastor focus of twelve to eighteen), we will work to see them integrated into our ministry and then handed on well into the next ministry.

5. <u>It shows we care about people</u>

Caring about people and families is a core ingredient to relational discipleship. Focusing on transitions, demonstrates that people are more important than programs. We are making investments that will shape a person for the long term.

How do you transition young people through your next generation ministries?

Transitions: Kids Ministry to Youth Ministry

We've looked at the importance of working across the next generation ministry (birth to 30 years) as a whole and seen why it's so important to align our teams around transitions. Now I want to break it down and explore what this looks like as a young person moves from kid's ministry to youth ministry. That is, the transition from primary school to year seven that happens at around twelve years of age.

I am so thankful for the amazing children and youth leaders[68] I have journeyed with in ministry, as they have shaped in me some important factors in terms of transitions from kid's ministry into youth ministry. Here are my top three tips for this transition.

1. Have a Feeder Pathway into Youth

By this I mean an opportunity for young people and families to engage with the rhythm of youth before they begin. This is done well at Crossway where this transition process begins in year five with the kid's ministry team running a fortnightly leadership development program on the same night as youth ministry. This is a two year rolling program, but it helps families move from a Sunday only rhythm to bring in Friday nights as well. This is only for a percentage of young people but it does make a difference.

---

[68] I am grateful for Narelle Ball (Golden Grove Baptist), Margaret Spicer (Crossway Baptist), and Michelle Stevens (Clovercrest Baptist) for shaping my thinking and practice around transitions from kid's ministry to youth ministry.

2. Have Regular Relational Connection Points

In the second half of year six, it's a great strategy for the Youth Pastor and some key volunteers to go along to kids' ministry from time to time (approximately once a month) and intentionally hang out with the year six group. You can play games, run and sit in on small group time, learning as many names as possible and basically building relationships. This makes the year sixers feel safe as they meet people they will see at youth group. The relational connection is significant here.

In term four the Youth Pastor and key volunteers could attend kids' ministry weekly for the first half of the term to really increase the relational connection. Hopefully by this stage this can include a volunteer leader or two that have already signed up to be year seven life group leaders for the following year. This sort of relational connect is priceless and if this can happen, it's a huge win.

To further relational connections, over the summer break, leaders could be encouraged to informally connect with youth. When the next year launches, the new year sevens could be invited to arrive early for the first three weeks to connect, meet their leaders, and generally feel safe in their new environment.

3. Celebrate Publicly

Transitions need to be celebrated publicly. One great way to do this is by having a graduation for the year sixes, as they move from kids' ministry and into youth ministry. This could happen on a youth night to help the process of families finding the new rhythm of youth. Or, it could happen in church on a Sunday, celebrating with the church community.

I promise you that if you provide a feeder pathway, relational connections and celebrate the transition publicly, this will result in a significantly higher sticking rate of young people from kid's ministry into youth ministry.

What great ideas do you have to transition young people from kids' ministry to youth?

Transitions: Youth Ministry to Young Adults Ministry

Youth are often compared to sheep because they love to stick together. However, young adults are more like cats in how they go their own way in thought and action.[69] This can make for a tricky

[69] Tim Hein mentioned this during an informal chat, in 2009. Tim is a brilliant thinker and speaker and I'm blessed to call him a friend.

transition from youth to young adults, but regardless of age, all have a desire to belong. Therefore relationships, community and life groups are all key ingredients in the transition process.[70]

During my time at Crossway I participated in a really successful transition program from youth ministry to young adult ministry, which is worth outlining here. On this model, formal year twelve transition into the young adults' ministry begins at the annual youth camp in July. The young adult team is invited to join the week-long camp and all the year twelves go to an elective called "leaving the cocoon" that is run by the young adults' team. This is a time to connect and get to know some of the young adult leaders, hear about the young adults' ministry from the people who run it, and build relationships over good coffee and food. In addition, the young adults' team lead year twelve discussion groups and intentionally spend informal time getting to know the year twelve crew.

During term four, the young adult leadership team mobilises the whole church in prayer for year twelves. They also put together

[70] The process being described here was developed and refined with the ideas of staff and key volunteers at Crossway from 2010 to 2014. Special mention goes to Leanne Hill and Andrew Simpson with whom I worked closely during this time, as we developed transitions from youth ministry to young adults' ministry.

exam survival packs which they give out in person at the regular senior youth night. This is another good opportunity to build profile for the next ministry stage.

As well as this, throughout the year a young adults' leader informally meets up with the year twelves to build connections, hear their stories, listen to their hopes and dreams, and also to share about the young adults' ministry. One year a leader arranged a pizza all you can eat day out, which was lots of fun and a masterstroke in building relationships and community.

The following year (that is, first year university / college / work) the young adult leaders follow up each school leaver and invite them along to a launch event such as a barbecue, coffee chat or beach day. Whatever it is, the aim is to connect the new young adults into community and especially into a life group.

One of the young adult staff members told me that since they began to go harder on the relational edge of follow up and meeting with young people to help them transition in, they have seen a 90% transition rate from year twelve into young adult life groups.[71]

[71] Informal conversation with Andrew Simpson, Young Adult Pastor at Crossway Baptist Church, 2012.

Wow! That is a huge result, especially when church attendance and faith development is generally falling off a cliff for this age group.

How is your faith community navigating transitions for youth into young adults' ministry? What barriers are you facing and how are you overcoming them?

Smooth Transitions

Possibly the most important factor in setting your ministry up for a massive win with transitions is a clean database.

Relationships are crucial, strategy is key, next generation staff alignment is so important, but, if you don't have a clean and functional database it can all be for nothing. Maintaining a clean database is one of the biggest challenges for churches of all sizes. Church can be a transient place, so keeping on top of who is who in the zoo, so to speak, is vital.

My advice is to have a system that works for the whole church.

Begin with the dream of having a whole church database system. If that won't work, then at least try to get alignment amongst the children's, youth and young adults' teams. Have a database that is easy to access, easy to update and can serve the ministry and not hinder it.

Whether you choose to use an excel spreadsheet or pay for an imported product, you need to have accurate names and contact details and a way of knowing who is regular, who isn't, and who might need some extra care. There is nothing worse than having a seventy-five-year-old lady on your year seven boys' list. (Insert awkward follow up conversation here!)

One approach is to categorise people on your database as active or inactive. This helps leaders to follow up youth, and sets the team up for a win when young people are transitioning into new ministries.

We so desire to see our young people grow in Jesus. For this to happen well, we need to be following them up and integrating them into community. To this end, a clean database will serve you well.

LEVERAGING PEAK EXPERIENCES

The Weapon of Camps

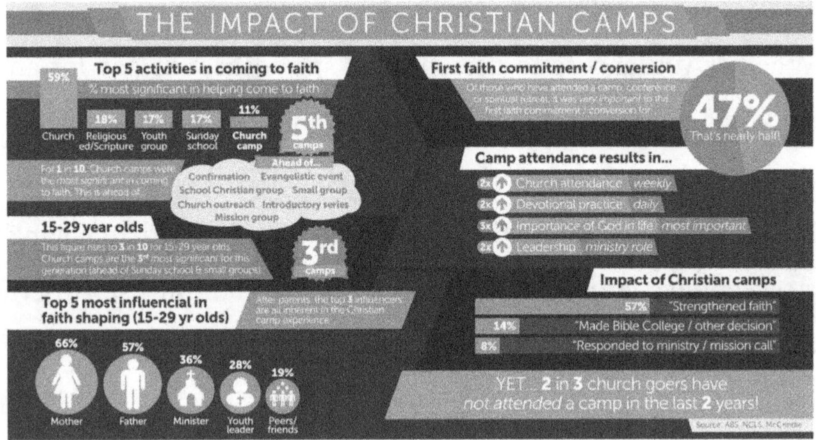

See Appendix 2 for larger graphic

A youth ministry friend recently showed me this infographic[72] that immediately got my attention. It is a great bit of research and confirms for many what they already know: camps and peak experiences are vital in youth ministry. They are, in fact, one of our best weapons in sowing and reaping gospel outcomes.

[72] http://www.christianvenues.org.au/impact/images/CVA_Infographic.pdf accessed 14/04/2017, used with permission

The research found that 47% of young people attending camps said that it was very important for them in making a decision for Jesus. This is a huge statistic. It's also a massive win that the momentum beyond camp attendance resulted in greater church attendance, Biblical engagement, awareness of God in the everyday, and leadership.

I think anyone who runs camps, senses this data intuitively. This is why we give so much to creating and running life-changing camps. But for those who don't run them, I would seriously ask you to consider these statistics. This highlights for me the importance of camps in the yearly rhythm of a youth ministry calendar, and brings into focus the why behind the what that is the purpose of camps.

I would encourage you to think seriously about the momentum of your annual calendar and strategically place your camp at a time when you can build momentum up to it and lever the maximum momentum out of it. Is it the start of the year to kick things off, mid-year when it gets cold and people get a bit sad due to the weather, or in the time before exams when you can celebrate what God has done throughout the year? Think about what works best in your local context.

I would also encourage you to always make time and space on camp for young people to respond to the gospel. It might sound simple, but it's so important to actively engage them in corporate gatherings, small group experiences and even one-on-one time, to ask them about life and faith and give them a chance for a genuine heart felt response.

I also urge you to make sure you take the camp experience into the home. Always keep in mind that parents are the primary disciplers. Mobilising them to continue the conversation will have lasting benefits.

For example, one idea that might help is to invite parents to an information session half an hour before the youth return from camp. Send back one or two of your most competent leaders and arm them with some highlights / challenges / funny stories from camp. Then give the parents two or three lead-in questions from the camp's teaching or experiences, which can foster and develop faith conversations in the home once the young person has recovered from camp.

Christian camps are important, don't take my word for it, trust the research! The big question is, how will you leverage this information to build your youth ministry?

Creating Memorable Camps

We know that camps are significant in enabling gospel outcomes. However, creating memorable camps is quite an art form and one that takes much hard work and planning.

My six keys for creating memorable camps are:

1. Have a core team

You can't lead anything of significance alone. To create a memorable camp a core team is essential, with different leaders having responsibility for various ministry portfolios. This may include: Camp Director, Administration, Community, Worship, Prayer, Logistics, and Discipleship. A role description for each core team member helps to give clarity and releases people with authority to fulfil their role right from the beginning of the planning process.

2. Have a theme running through the camp

I am a massive fan of trying to run a theme through the different elements of camp. I believe this adds to the overall experience. The one caveat to be aware of is it must be done well. It needs to be thoroughly planned and executed well, so that it adds to the camp and doesn't detract from it. One year our theme was

Kingdom and this ran through the worship and teaching and into the tribal wars and community games. We had kings and queens on each tribe and the theme weaved beautifully through different elements of camp.

3. Cultivate invested leaders

It's important to have a rigorous leadership selection process to ensure you have leaders with the best character, who are heavily invested in serving young people. Look for leaders who set an example and are genuine role models to the young people, as they participate in worship and learning, and also in getting messy in games. To run a memorable camp, be ruthless in only inviting invested leaders who love Jesus and are committed to serving Him and the young people.

4. Enable multiple connection points for campers

It's vital to have multiple points of contact for a camper to belong and feel part of the experience. As all people are unique, so too will be their connection into camp. It's our responsibility as the leadership team to create an environment which fosters a sense of belonging. Multiple connection points can include tribal war games, singing worship, creative worship, personal camper quiet time, electives, guys / girls chats, night life experiences (such as bonfire, dance party, glow in the dark sports), main stage teaching, life groups, nightly dorm devotions, and simple free time. Have a look at your camp program and see if you have multiple connection points woven throughout the experience.

5. Foster memory makers

Think back to camps you attended and camps you now run. What stays with you? It's no surprise that memory makers are such an important aspect in creating memorable camps! Whether it's running the gauntlet with young people throwing oversized exercise balls at your head, an annual game, some inflatable fun (such as zorb or walking on water balls), pranks, pumping worship, Christ candle, student stories and more. Memory makers are essential and you need to plan for them!

6. Follow up

Thorough post camp follow up is essential. Ask campers to fill in a response card on the last day. Look for key statistics such as first time commitment, recommitment, interest in baptism, and perhaps, "What is a key question you would like to be asked following this camp?" Ensure your team relationally follows up each camper within the week if possible. Follow up is important, therefore make sure you plan for it so that you execute it well.

Camps are significant in the spiritual formation of young people. My encouragement and challenge to you is to plan well and create the most memorable camp possible. Write down some of your key elements in creating memorable camps and reflect on why they work so well.

Why You Need a Family Camp

I had just returned from a family camp. I was tired, my head hurt, I had nothing left to give but somehow my heart was so full. I was smiling and energised in my privileged role of serving God.

Pitched to families in the church as, **"A long weekend with a long-term impact"**,[73] registrations were limited to the first thirty families to sign up. Camp was aimed at families with primary aged children and, due to a cap on numbers, this restricted scale added value to the camp's all-important relational edge.

We asked the congregation to sponsor families who couldn't afford it, recognising that this stage is probably the time where families

[73] Thanks to Margaret Spicer from Crossway Baptist who was the main driver behind Family Camp experiences.

have the least amount of disposable income but need a camp like this to connect and refuel. The church responded and over $10,000 came in, which meant that many families who desired to go but couldn't afford it were able to come along. It looks like the wider church also saw the value in the camp!

It was amazing! We had all-in family worship experiences, parent only sessions, kid time, solid practical teaching, guys went and played ten pin bowling and table tennis, girls had a coffee and chat night, we had beach time as families, late night cards, and more.

We empowered the parents to parent, and this helped a lot with discipline issues. We tried to have a balance of formal and informal time, and kept the structure open and flexible. We brought along some extra helpers to run the kids' time, which was a huge win.

We had some single parents come to camp and to help bring the right level of support for them, we invited two couples along so that when we asked parents to "walk and talk" on a certain issue, they had someone to walk with, too.

Another thing I loved about family camp was working with our Children and Young Families Pastor to organise the event, and we also invited our Young Adults Pastor along. My family was an active part of the weekend, making it extra special, and as a church leadership team we modelled generational ministry and connection and the value of family.

As a pastor, husband, father and disciple of Jesus, it was so great to see families connecting with God and with other families. One dad said to me on the final day, **"Thanks so much for organising this. We needed it so much as a family and I needed it as a dad."** Enough said; there is a win right there.

How could you include a family camp in your annual ministry rhythm? What is one step you could do this week to make this idea become a reality?

CAMPS ARE SIGNIFICANT IN THE SPIRITUAL
FORMATION OF YOUNG PEOPLE.

BIG EVENTS

Why Big Events Still Have a Place

When I was a teenager my church held big outreach events. I have planned and run them too as a volunteer and paid Youth Pastor, and I know they will continue to have an important place in the landscape of youth ministry moving forward. This is why.

Big events reach into the local community

Big events help keep the focus of making disciples the main game. They give a great opportunity to think outside the four walls of the church building to develop relationships with local schools and invite young people along to youth group. A clear gospel message with an opportunity for response, provides a platform for youth to choose Jesus.

Big events give youth an entry into outreach

If you asked a young person as their first step to share their faith or open the Bible with a mate, most of them would freak out. But, having an entry level challenge of inviting a mate along to a youth group night – which will be fun and where there will be a God spot – is actually achievable. This builds confidence in young people and sets them up for future wins.

Big events are fun

Nerf wars, dance parties, scavenger hunts, water fight nights, academy awards nights, push-kart races… come on! Large scale big events are so much fun! I have often had parents want to come along and be teenagers again when we run big events. They are fun and wild and this is an element we need to keep fostering in our young people and our ministries.

Big events develop momentum

Big events do something in the lives of the youth but also the leaders. They bring a sense of excitement, seeing teenagers coming to Christ builds faith in the entire group, leaders working together on something big fosters unity, and there seems to be a natural momentum for the rest of the term out of big events.

Big events foster partnership

Over the years, I have loved working with a wide range of churches to pull together big events. We have done regional events and have partnered with other churches and para-church organisations. This is very healthy as it helps your leaders and youth connect to a much bigger story of God that is happening across your state or even nation. Partnership is essential in the advancement of the gospel and big events are a platform for greater influence and growth as churches work and learn together.

List below some of the best big events you have been involved in over the journey.

How to Run a Big Event

The first thing to recognise is that you can't run a big event alone. You need a team of committed leaders who can all play their role to make the night a success. This team might come from your church or, if you are running a regional youth event, the team could be comprised of all the churches represented. From my experience a team should consist of:

- Team leader: The person to run point in the lead up planning phase and also during the event itself.

- Promotions leader: The person who organises print (event flyers, posters, etc.) and online (social media channels, etc.) promotions for the event and ensures it's easy for young people to invite their friends along.

- Activities leader: The person who designs the activities and major elements of the night.

- Registration leader: The person who receives payments, helps get the youth into the building and allocates them into teams.

- Hospitality leader: If you run a café or supper post activities, you need someone running point on this.

- Set up and pack down leader: It's vital to have designated people on set up and pack down.

- Communicator and gospel response leader: Having a gospel message that links into the theme of the night is essential. It's also vital to have a team of leaders who see who is responding and follow them up personally after the talk.

Planning for a big event needs to begin months out in broad ideas. As it gets closer, more specific details need to be sorted and jobs allocated. This will take time and planning, so there is no way you can run a big event without meetings.

During the week leading into a big event, it is smart to ask your leaders if they have any spare time to come into the office to help with preparations. Also, on the day before the event or on the day itself (depending on people's availability and the church space availability) make a lot of noise setting up as a team. This will help your leaders grow in a sense of excitement and anticipation around the big event as well. The strategy of asking everyone and then tapping a few individuals on the shoulder to see if they can help, usually works in getting enough people mobilised in the setting up process.

From my experience the best rhythm for big events is two per term. It's important to promote them as outreach nights and mobilise your young people to invite their friends. I have often used the line with the youth, "Outreach nights are not for you, they are for your mates who don't know Jesus yet." We know they will be heaps of fun and everyone will enjoy them, but the main purpose is to share the gospel in a creative way and give young people the opportunity to respond to Jesus. Therefore, the message and response is a key part of the night. The way I see big events is like a funnel: start wide and fun, slowly get more serious and pointed as the night goes on and then have the message and response.

Once the night is over and you have packed down and everyone is feeling both tired and satisfied at the same time, the best thing to do is to go out for some food and celebrate! Go to your local café or hamburger place; whichever is open at the potentially late hour. Invite all the leaders and tell stories of funny moments. Also share what God was up to during the night in the lives of the young people who responded to the message.

How do you use big events in the rhythm of your youth ministry?

... BUT THE MAIN PURPOSE IS TO SHARE THE GOSPEL IN A CREATIVE WAY AND GIVE YOUNG PEOPLE THE OPPORTUNITY TO RESPOND TO JESUS.

If relationship is the glue and leadership is the applicator, **these youth ministry essentials are the surfaces to be stuck together**. These are the critical areas of relational engagement that we must respond to as we consider the uniqueness of: the individual (formation), their influencers (parents and peers), and how they respond to a change in rhythm (transitions and events).

I see embracing these essentials, as a refusal to be taken by surprise through ignorance, but rather to recognise what is coming and take proactive steps. I am also convinced that these essentials could be synonymous with "greatest challenges," for in as much as we seek to understand and respond to them, they are forever changing and evolving with society. Perhaps this is why we often relegate them to the margins of our time: even as we recognise that a spontaneous approach has had little effect in the past, the discipline of planning always feels like we are left chasing a moving target.

I remember sitting down with Mike after working on our life group cultures. There was a strong sense of, "If we don't decide where we want to go, we will only be swept along." We needed some strategic targets that could be observed without becoming obsolete. What surprised me was how tangible these desired cultures ultimately were when relational discipleship was at our core. Yet this was only one area of relational engagement, and limited as Mike highlighted, to that forty structured hours of exposure we had on average with a young person each year. To expand the essentials, and embrace a parent partnership model was an intimidating, necessary, and natural next step for us.

As you read through these essentials – **what is the intimidating, necessary, and natural next relational area for you to engage?**

- **Developing a Discipleship Culture**
- **Partnering with Parents**
- **Leveraging Peak Experiences**
- **Establishing a Life Group Model**
- **Managing Transitions**

To bring about strategic change in these areas simultaneously would only be cause for chaos, but to focus on each of these areas over time creates increasing potential for the glue of relationship to holistically engage with each unique young person.

With this in mind, is it any wonder that camp experiences are so impacting given the way they can envelop these essentials? For our annual Winter Camp, this was a combination of big memorable games, daily life groups, a Year 6 invitation to a day of camp, teaching that moved youth to respond, and arranging to meet with the parents before youth return to answer questions and continue engagement in the home. It should come as no surprise that this is a highlight of each year.

When I see the relationship, the leadership, and a proactive approach to essentials align, everything inside me delights – when a life group leader of a freshly transitioned Year 7 student tells me that they have been invited over for dinner by the parent of that youth – they must wonder why I high-five them so hard!

MAKE THE GLUE STICK

1.   If I had to distribute ten points to these three aspects of discipleship, where would I allocate them according to the strengths and weaknesses of **my current ministry?**

   Head (Knowing)   **Heart (Being)**   **Hands (Doing)**

2.   If I had to distribute ten points to these three aspects of discipleship, where would I allocate them according to the strengths and weaknesses of **my personal faith?**

   Head (Knowing)   **Heart (Being)**   **Hands (Doing)**

Is there anything I should reflect on because of what I see above?

3.   As I consider the importance of life groups for a relational approach to discipleship, where would I plot my current ministry on this continuum?

More time in Rows   **More time in Circles**

<-- -->

4.   Are there any changes I need to make to recalibrate this? Who do I need to speak to?

☐   my supervisor

☐   my team

☐   an external mentor

☐   my Lead Pastor

(Send them a text message right now.)

The nature of anything essential is that it is a factor whether we choose to acknowledge it or not. Considering this power, we should treat these essentials as opportunities to be leveraged with care: each a poem to interpret, not a puzzle to complete.

THINK

What is our rate of
retention between Year 6
and starting youth?
Are youth falling
through the gap?

Is there a creative way
we can get parents to
connect with the leader
of their child?

Are there cultures that we
can articulate and pursue
over the next three years?

ACT

Gather missing parent
contact information.

Allocate some additional
funds to ensure a big
event is a memorable one.

Multiply (split) larger life
groups to ensure there is
a maximum
of 6-8 members.

FUTURE FOCUS

Do you ever wonder what the future will look like? What crazy things will be part of our world. In recent years Apple, Facebook, Uber, and Airbnb are examples of how we have changed the way we engage and interact. We live in a rapidly changing world and it feels like things are speeding up as I get older!

When it comes to youth ministry, what will the future look like? Great question. The truth is no one really knows. But what I am committed to, in the words of Andy Stanley, is to "Marry the mission but date the method."[74] In the future I hope methods change, but we will stay focused on loving God, loving people, and making disciples.[75] I truly believe that relational discipleship is a Kingdom way of doing life and reaching people for Jesus.

[74] Andy Stanley, 284.

[75] Matthew 22: 36-40 and Matthew 28: 18-20

This section will explore insights around the future and how we can best navigate the terrain ahead. These insights include:

1: *INTERGENERATIONAL FORMATION*

2: *HEALTHY INTERGENERATIONAL MINISTRIES*

3: *FINISHING A ROLE WELL*

4: *MAINTAINING THE LIGHT ON THE HILL*

INTERGENERATIONAL FORMATION

I don't know if you have realised but most youth leaders are only just adults themselves. Don't get me wrong, their relatability and enthusiasm for life is great. However, if we aren't careful we could find ourselves in a situation where we have a generation discipling the same generation. This would be a narrow approach to discipleship.

One of my all-time favourite youth leaders was Sandy. She was a mum in her middle years and she was such an effective youth leader. She didn't try to be cool but instead she simply loved the youth and was a consistent godly presence in their lives. She embodied relational discipleship and was a great example of an intergenerational leader. She had the desire and ability to cross the generations and our youth group was so much richer for it.

Intergenerational ministry is part of the future of youth ministry. What could this look like?

What are intergenerational relationships?

Allen and Ross in their research offer up these two compelling quotes: "Intergenerational most often describes a church that intentionally cultivates meaningful interaction between generations."[76] And, "Intergenerational ministry occurs when a congregation intentionally brings the generations together in mutual serving, sharing or learning within the core activities of the church, to live out being the body of Christ to each other and the greater community."[77]

From oldest to youngest the generations are: Builders, Baby Boomers, Generation X, Generation Y or Millennials, and Generation Z. For the first time in history we have five generations in the marketplace and four generations in the workforce. The opportunity in front of us is to help cultivate meaningful relationships and interactions between the generations.

Why are we talking about intergenerational relationships?

Allen and Ross state, "For a variety of reasons the church has

[76] Holly Allen and Christine Ross, *Intergenerational Christian Formation: Bringing The Whole Church Together in Ministry, Community and Worship* (Downers Grove, Illinois: IVP Academic, 2012), 19.

[77] Holly Allen and Christine Ross, 17.

increasingly moved towards the segregation of people by ages and life stages. However, our research indicates that frequent cross-generational experiences are essential to Christian formation and the development of mature faith."[78]

Basically, younger people are growing up in church environments in which they don't know adults like they did in years gone past. For example, in one church known to me the young people don't come into a church service until they are in high school. Also, there can be an unhealthy mindset in some churches that, "If kids are quiet then the children's pastor is doing a good job" and therefore limited cultivation of relationships between generations occurs. It also needs to be noted that tougher child protection laws (which are good and right) have created a barrier between generations and we need to rethink the best way to naturally connect across the generations.

What does the Bible say about intergenerational formation?

The Bible tells us to pass on our faith from one generation to the next. Psalm 71 says, "Even when I am old and grey, do not forsake

[78] Holly Allen and Christine Ross, 25.

me, my God, till I declare your power to the next generation, your mighty acts to all who are to come."[79] Who is the next generation mentioned in this Psalm? Simply, it is anyone that will live longer than you and me!

The Apostle Paul when speaking to his younger prodigy Timothy put it this way, "You then, my son, be strong in the grace that is in Christ Jesus. And the things you have heard me say in the presence of many witnesses entrust to reliable people who will also be qualified to teach others."[80] We have a responsibility to entrust the next generation to teach others. They will only be able to do this if we help them become reliable.

What does the research say about intergenerational formation?

The Barna Group discovered that intergenerational relationships are a "big deal to both engaged and unengaged young adults."[81] This was found to be both positive and negative. Positive for those who felt welcomed and engaged, and negative for those who were disengaged and who felt judged and isolated.

[79] Psalm 71:18

[80] 2 Timothy 2:1-2

[81] Barna Group. "Young Adult Study". Ventura, California, 2013. http://www.youngadultlife.com/wp-content/uploads/2015/01/Barna-SDA-Millennials-Report-final.pdf, 48.

In his research, Chuck Bomar found that intergenerational relationships "sound great"[82] but can be difficult to cultivate and maintain. Millennials value intentionality without over-structuring and desire a deep level of authenticity. This can be hard to find in older people. Bomar states, "To effectively navigate a relationship with a college-aged person you should have only one agenda: to get to know the person"[83], and "Unfortunately I find a lack of older adults who authentically experience God daily."[84]

Are intergenerational relationships on your radar? Do you see them as important in reaching and discipling young people?

WE HAVE A RESPONSIBILITY TO ENTRUST THE NEXT GENERATION TO TEACH OTHERS.

---

[82] Chuck Bomar, *Worlds Apart: Understanding the Mindset and Values of 18-25 year olds,* (Grand Rapids, Michigan, Zondervan, 2011), 141.

[83] Chuck Bomar, 142.

[84] Chuck Bomar, , 146.

HEALTHY INTERGENERATIONAL MINISTRIES

If intergenerational relationships are a missing piece in our youth ministry landscape, then what are some practices we can explore to increase their prevalence? I propose the following four strategies as a good starting point.

1. Develop Mentoring Relationships

The current research points to the significance of older people in the lives of younger people for positive faith formation. The Barna Group state, "Millennials need the help of faithful believers from older generations if they are to make sense of it all and move meaningfully forward in their life and faith."[85] Life-on-life mentoring is as important now as it ever was. Growing up these days is complex and can be difficult. Young people need mentoring in all areas of their lives.

The Fuller Youth Institute research that recommended five significant adults in the life of one young person[86] is as relevant

[85] Barna Group. "5 Reasons Millennials Stay Connected to Church". September 2013, accessed 14/4/2017. https://www.barna.org/barna-update/millennials/635-5-reasons-millennials-stay-connected-to-church#.V6awzuh97IU, 10.

[86] Dr Kara Powell, Brad Griffin and Dr Cheryl Crawford, *Sticky Faith: Youth Worker Ed* (Grand Rapids, Michigan: Zondervan, 2011), 79.

now as it was five years ago. Think Orange's work around "widening the circle"[87] in parenting and a young person's development is essential. The old proverb, "It takes a village to raise a child" is still pertinent. Effective mentoring is essential, for us to train and develop the next generation in the right way to go.

This research is even more significant if we look at what is happening in our world from a generational change perspective. Mark McCrindle states that by 2020, 42% of the workforce in Australia will consist of Generation Y. Our nation will be undergoing generational change in the form of the largest intergenerational wealth transfer and the biggest leadership succession and handover ever seen.[88] For this to go well, older leaders will need to embrace this change and, as they step aside from formal work duties, lead and mentor a new generation into the future.

---

[87] Reggie Joiner and Carey Nieuwhof, *Parenting Beyond Your Capacity: Connect Your Family to a Wider Community* (Colorado Springs, USA: David Cook Distribution, 2010), 57-81.

[88] McCrindle Research. "Australia in 2020: A Snapshot of the Future". Accessed 14/4/2017. http://mccrindle.com.au/ResearchSummaries/Australia-in-2020-A-Snapshot-of-the-Future.pdf, 1.

A growing idea amongst Millennials is what is known as reverse mentoring.[89] Young people want to be taken seriously and to contribute. Reverse mentoring describes a kind of give and take between younger leaders (who are at ease with modern technology and can teach others) and established leaders (who share wisdom from years in the trenches).

How can you develop intentional mentoring relationships in your ministry?

To finish off this thought, let's do a pairing exercise (just like Bluetooth). Who in your church could be paired up relationally? How could you make it happen?

[89] Barna Group. "5 Reasons Millennials Stay Connected to Church". September 2013, accessed 14/4/2017. https://www.barna.org/barna-update/millennials/635-5-reasons-millennials-stay-connected-to-church#.V6awzuh97IU

2. Have Life Groups

I have already written about the importance of life groups. Now and into the future we need to be committed to creating smaller relational circles from a young age. Having a significant adult walking alongside younger people is essential in fostering intergenerational relationships and effective faith development.

The Barna Group state that room needs to be made for meaningful relationships if the next generation are going to grow in their faith.[90] This demonstrates the importance of authentic relationships as a foundation for faith formation. I believe that life groups are the best vehicle for this to occur.

I can see the importance of life groups across the generations through the life of one young man, Sam. Sam is an exceptional young man who leads in our youth ministry; he is a life group leader who cares for up to eight Year 7 boys. Sam is also in a life group and is growing and being nurtured by a couple in their mid-forties. Sam cares for people and he, himself, is being cared for by people. This is the way it should be in the Kingdom of God, and life groups facilitate the process.

[90] Barna Group. "5 Reasons Millennials Stay Connected to Church". September 2013, accessed 14/4/2017. https://www.barna.org/barna-update/millennials/635-5-reasons-millennials-stay-connected-to-church#.V6awzuh97IU

Do you create a learning environment of rows or circles? What is one thing you can do to move towards a circle culture?

____

____

3. Empower Families

We have spent a portion of section 3 on partnering with parents, demonstrating the importance of this. It is true that parents are the primary disciplers and key influencers of their children,[91] and this is both a current and future issue. So the question is, how do we help them step into this high calling?

Below are a number of ways you can empower families:

- Pray for them: Set reminders in your phone to pray for marriages and families.

- Provide regular discipleship material: Such as take home sheets.

- Communicate often: At least weekly with an email or SMS.

[91] Dr Kara Powell, Brad Griffin and Dr Cheryl Crawford, *Sticky Faith: Youth Worker Ed* (Grand Rapids, Michigan: Zondervan, 2011), 116-117.

- Provide training: Train parents irregularly but with the best material. Our highest attended training event was an adolescent development session.

- Create opportunities for shared serving: Such as family mission trips.

How are you empowering your families for the high calling of discipling their children?

4. Use GQ in Leadership Development of Younger Leaders

You would have heard of IQ (intellectual intelligence) and EQ (emotional intelligence), and now there is GQ (generational intelligence). Haydn Shaw has written a wonderfully thoughtful and positive book on understanding how different people from different generations connect with God in unique ways.[92] Like I mentioned previously it is the first time in history that we have five generations in the marketplace and four in the workforce, and

---

[92] Shaw, Haydn. Generation IQ: *Christianity Isn't Dying, Millennials Aren't the Problem, And the Future is Bright.* Carol Stream, Illinois: Tyndale House Publishers, 2015.

we need to be considerate and thoughtful about how we develop this next generation.

Mark McCrindle offers these thoughts on leading the next generation:[93]

- Move from "knowing the way" to "showing the way". Instead of command and control leadership, Millenials respond better to consensus and collaborative leadership.

- Adopt a people-centered approach to leadership. When Gen Ys were asked what qualities they valued most in their leaders, they responded with: honesty, reliability, loyalty, energetic, team focused and inspiring.

- Move from IQ to EQ. Millenials respond more effectively to leaders who have EQ. Therefore, develop emotional intelligence among the leaders in your organisation.

[93] Mark McCrindle, The ABC of XYZ: *Understanding the Global Generations* (Sydney, NSW: UNSW Press, 2011), 175.

How are you growing in your leadership so that you can lead the next generation?

FINISHING A ROLE WELL

In finishing my role as Lead Youth Pastor at Crossway Baptist Church in Melbourne, I felt so blessed by the way the Crossway leadership team empowered me to run hard until the finish line. Throughout the process I learnt much about finishing well. If you are in ministry, at some point into the future, you will need to know how to finish well. Here are my top five tips.

1. Make and Stick to a Plan

The stage at which you bring your Senior Pastor into your discernment process will be determined by the level of your relationship. I was fortunate to have a healthy and trusting relationship with my Senior Pastor, so I included him from the beginning. Once you have involved them and have made the decision to move on, together you need to make a plan for when you will inform the wider community. It is one thing to make a plan; you also need to ensure you stick to it.

I found creating a timeline of events was helpful in sharing the news in a way that honoured those closest to me, but also held others in appropriate relationship. In my context, that meant telling my youth staff, then key staff at church, followed by key youth volunteers, and then, in a blast of a weekend, the youth, parents and wider church.

2. Invest In Relationships

What do you want to be known for? What will be your leaving gift to the church? Answering these two questions will determine what legacy you want to leave in your current setting. The answer for me was and always will be, relationships.

Do you think your church wants another program or initiative just when you have decided to leave? I encourage you to invest in what lasts: people. Spend time supporting and encouraging each of your leaders, key youth and families, and other key relationships in the life of the church and community. I did this and I have no regrets. People matter, and discipleship happens best through relationship, so when you finish up, finish well with people by continuing to invest into relationships.

3. Be Extra Gracious

One thing you will find, when you announce that you're leaving, is that some people will withdraw from the relationship. Some people will begin to exclude you from the decision-making process and others will just stop engaging with you. It is easy to take this personally because we work in such highly relational environments, but don't take offence. It is actually right and healthy for the organisation moving forward to do this.

A wise friend of mine said, "Mike, one tip to finishing well is being extra gracious."[94] This was seriously great advice. It helped me to navigate some potentially sticky moments when I felt the pains of transition. It's important to remember that you have chosen to move on and therefore the responsibility lies with you to show extra grace.

4. Be Present and Push Hard

In the interval between the announcement that you are leaving and your actual finishing date, it is important to fight the urge to look to your next ministry assignment. It's imperative that you stay present and push hard to the end. You don't want to be that

---

[94] This friend is a business leader who was transitioning roles at the same time as me and I'm thankful for his generosity into my life.

guy or girl that people said had checked out and didn't finish well. I can honestly say I have no regrets about my time finishing at Crossway, as I pushed hard loving the people God put in front of me right until the end of my time.

I took some time off between roles and only then did I let my head and heart dream and go to what was ahead. Be present and push hard to the end!

5. Have a Memorable Finish

I thought in advance about how I was going to finish with different people and teams. I had some one-on-one catch ups with key people and a dinner with my core team, but it was on my final night at youth group that I wanted to do something a little memorable. Instead of preaching a regular message, I wrote my youth group an open letter, inspired by Rob Bell's effort when he finished at Mars Hill.[95] It began with some thanks, then I shared a lesson they had taught me, gave some warnings for us all, and ended with a confession. It was a special time and I spoke from the heart with the intention of depositing hope and a future into the young crew coming through.

---

[95] See: https://sojo.net/articles/rob-bells-parting-epistle-mars-hill-grace-peace

If you are finishing up or in the beginning stages of transition, how can you leave well and leave behind a legacy of life and hope that reflects Jesus?

MAINTAINING THE LIGHT ON THE HILL

Is the Church in Australia Becoming Invisible?

China hit the news recently as researchers anticipate it being the "most Christian nation" within the next fifteen years,[96] surpassing the United States with a whopping 247 million Christians by 2030! It is great to see the church explode in China and I praise God for this. But, as I think about our little pond called Australia, it makes me stop and ask the following questions. Where is the gospel placed in Australia? Where is the church really at in Australia? How is the gospel advancing in our wonderful nation? You might want to ask these questions of the current setting where you serve God.

[96] http://www.telegraph.co.uk/news/worldnews/asia/china/10776023/China-on-course-to-become-worlds-most-Christian-nation-within-15-years.html accessed April 14, 2017.

McCrindle research[97] shows us that the rate of Australians identifying themselves as Christian has been in steady decline over the last century, from 96% in 1911 to 61.1% in the 2011 census. Even in this last decade, statistics moved from 68% to 61.1%. On paper, Christianity is still Australia's largest religion. Twice the number of Australians attend church than attend a football game of any code. However, church attendance has more than halved in the last four decades, from 36% in 1972 to 15% in 2014.

I know that there are some pockets and movements doing well in making disciples but **my fear is that Christianity is somewhat invisible to people outside** of our movements. For people outside of our Christian bubble – regular sport / family / gardening / coffee / beer / music / wine-loving people – do they know we exist and gather on a Sunday? Do they know we are just like them and love Jesus with all our hearts? Outside of our Christian circles, is the church becoming invisible? As I wrestle with the reality of this question, my deep fear is that the church is indeed becoming invisible to the average Australian.

I don't know about you but I don't want this steady decline to be the end of the story for faith development in Australia. **My heart**

[97] http://mccrindle.com.au/BlogRetrieve aspx?PostID=465624&A
=SearchResult&SearchID=7231166&ObjectID=465624&ObjectType=55

and desire is that God's name would be elevated in this great country of ours and our story would have a bright future with millions of Australians coming into relationship with the living Jesus. But for this to be the case, we must become proactive and work super hard in becoming visible. Jesus said that "We are the light of the world. A city on a hill cannot be hidden". We are light and we carry His light, so are we shining bright?

Contact > Connect > Communicate

A simple strategy to make us more visible is called the *Contact > Connect > Communicate*[98] continuum.

Contact: Be intentional in knowing your community and the key demographic make-up of the people in your unique patch of Australia. Contact them through both physical and digital mediums, being proactive in breaking down any perceived barriers that might exist between the local Australian and your church.

Connect: Have as many connection points as possible for people to explore your faith community. This may include special celebrations that are geared for "outsiders" at Easter and

[98] This is part of the 'Big Purpose' developed by Pastor Dale Stephenson at Crossway Baptist Church.

Christmas; regular spots on the radio or in the local paper; intentional acts of love and care in the local community, and large scale events for people of all ages to explore.

<u>Communicate</u>: Be clear about who you are and be intentional about introducing people to Jesus. It's important to help shape, and for some re-shape, their views on Jesus and open up avenues to have meaningful conversations. Sometimes this happens one-on-one and sometimes this happens from the platform, depending on the nature and purpose of the activity.

It's a very simple but profoundly strategic tool for making contact with our local community, connecting with them, and seeking out opportunities to communicate why we exist as a church. As I implemented this in youth ministry I found that **trust is built over time,** and barriers come down as relationship is fostered and cultivated.

Our challenge is to not let the church become invisible on our watch. It's our day, our time and our opportunity to meaningfully understand our local Australians and reach into their worlds with the life changing love of Jesus.

Think about your local area now. Do your local people even know your church exists? Why? What is one relational thing you could do this month to increase your visibility?

OUR CHALLENGE IS TO NOT LET THE CHURCH
BECOME INVISIBLE ON OUR WATCH.

If we want to ensure the glue sticks long-term, it all comes back to quality. The reason super-glue comes in such small tubes is because the manufacturer knows how powerful its adhesive properties are, while some surfaces need a special type of glue for adhesion to even occur! The same is true for relationships, and when it comes to the future of youth ministry, we are only just scratching the surface of this reality.

On various occasions in our teenage years, my future wife but girlfriend at the time, Megan and I would ditch youth group for the night to visit the older folk of our church and play Scrabble. They were not young, but they were young at heart, and I can still remember how delighted they were to have us there, yet in some mysterious way, we were the ones who walked away blessed. I sometimes wonder what our ministries would look like if every young person got to experience the kind of welcome that we did. Intergenerational ministry isn't just about connecting people of various life-stages, it is about the hospitality, the acceptance, the quality *glue* that comes with it.

The word "mentor" was foreign to me until many years after I had instinctively adopted this methodology as a teenager. School teachers, friends of my parents, and yes of course, youth leaders, all played a critical role in shaping my faith and leadership, but it was only in hindsight that I saw how they listened, cared, and drew the best out of me. It's a fascinating reminder that the appreciation of tomorrow is likely to be already in progress today. Take a moment to consider – **who is investing in *you* right now?**

	The Person	Their Investment in Me
1.		
2.		

While opportunities may be forged through structure, perhaps simply giving permission for young people to seek out people they connect and have chemistry with is the best way we can ensure a healthy future.

As a witness to the declining rate of people identifying as Christian in Australia, it could be easy to become intimidated or fearful of the future. In the face of that pressure, I'm reminded that we trust in a God who doesn't waste anything, and is committed to pruning back that which is both fruitless, and fruitful (John 15:2). In the same way we, as ministry leaders, should be unafraid to critique ourselves and ask the question, "Are we both meaningful and memorable in how we share the good news of Jesus?" It may just be that God wants to use these vulnerable moments to refine our vision, and open up new pathways for growth and fruitfulness.

Leaders may come and go, social conscience may shift, access may be denied, but the church will never become invisible if quality spirit-filled people are willing to reach into the lives of others through relationship, just as Jesus did. Disciples will multiply, and **the glue will stick.**

MAKE THE GLUE STICK

1.   What is one area I need to personally work on to make my **faith more visible?**

☐   **Contact: Knowing Your Community**

☐   **Connect: Engaging Your Community**

☐   **Communicate: Articulating Your Faith**

2.   What is the average age of my youth leadership team?

_________ **years**

3. As I consider the importance of intergenerational relationships as shaping the discipleship of youth, where would I plot
my church on this continuum?

Demographic Segregation   **Demographic Integration**

$\longleftarrow$ - $\longrightarrow$

4. Reflecting on the last two questions, are there any changes
we need to make as a church to recalibrate? Who do I need to
speak to first?

◻ my supervisor

◻ my team

◻ an external mentor

◻ my Lead Pastor

(Send them a text message right now.)

It is important to remember that intergenerational challenge can
and should be embraced in both directions. As young people
reach up for experience, the older generation can reach down
for potential – this is the church functioning at its best.

NEXT STEP

THINK

What unique qualities do other generations or life-stages have that our youth desperately need?

Is the future of the ministry dependent on me? Do I need to let go of anything?

How am I being a "light on the hill" to my neighbours?

ACT

Invite people you trust to be part of a prayer and intercession team for you.

Seek out a mentor who is deliberately different to you.

Recommend to church leadership that they invite a young leader to join or witness their conversations.

FINAL THOUGHTS

DISNEYLAND AND YOUTH MINISTRY

I want to come back to the importance of relational discipleship. To do this let me tell you about the first time I went to Disneyland. It took thirty-two years but I made it! In the words of some of my youth, "It was epic!" What a full-on fourteen hours of rides, fun, overpriced lunch, more rides, a night water show and then more rides and fun. As I immersed myself in the happy Disneyland / California Adventure Park experience, it taught me two things we can apply to keep relational discipleship at the core of our ministry practice.

1. The Power of a Story

Each ride has a story, with good and evil, humour and characters that draw you in to their world. The story is told in such a captivating way that it is memorable. Some of the rides tell stories that are familiar to us, like the Star Wars 3D ride, or the Indiana Jones, or the Pirates of the Caribbean rides. But over at California Adventure Park, the Hollywood Tower of Terror ride told a captivating story located in a hotel, ending with a… Well, you might just have to go there to get the ending!

It made me think, how well do we tell God's big story in youth ministry? How do we engage and captivate our young people with what God has done and is doing in our world? How do we use a multi-sensory approach that stays with our young people and is memorable? I ask these questions because stories are memorable, they work in communicating truth using a range of emotions.

2. The Power of The Personal Contact

Both theme parks were buzzing with friendly faces; those of both staff and famous Disney and Pixar characters. It was as if we had access to what we had previously only seen on TV or as a plush toy. I got a photo with Winnie the Pooh (for my son of course!), gave Buzz Lightyear a high five, and was surprised at how upbeat all the staff were. We were lining up for the evening water / light show and one of the staff asked if we were okay. When we mentioned that we were looking for a spot to view the show, she immediately began chatting to us and then walked us to a viewing area. She was in no rush; she was polite, kind, and appeared interested in knowing whether we had had a great day. I was impressed by her personal service and the way she went the extra mile without needing to.

This made me reflect on how important it is to value people over programs and to see the program as the vehicle in making and developing relationships. This was already a value in my youth ministry, but I was reminded how much we need to keep pushing this.

I hope by now that I've convinced you that relationship is the glue. It is the connection for an effective youth ministry. How we tell God's big story and invite young people into discipling relationships, is crucial in seeing God's Kingdom come on earth as it is in heaven. How is this a value for you personally? How is this reflected in your youth ministry?

Thank you, Disneyland, for demonstrating to me the power of the story and the power of personal contact. Who would have thought you might make me a more thoughtful and effective Youth Pastor!

Think about your youth ministry in the context of these two Disneyland insights on the power of story and personal contact. Do a quick audit and ask yourself if there is an area where you can make a change to increase your ministry effectiveness? What is it and why? Write them below.

Story:

____

____

____

____

Personal Contact:

____

____

____

____

KEY IDEAS

David Stark says, "we remember 5% of what we hear, 10% of what we see, 25% of what we read, 55% of what we discuss, 65% of what we help create or experience with others, and 95% of what we teach others."[99] My hope and desire is that you have read and learnt some things in the preceding pages of this book. But to truly embed key ideas and principles into your life and ministry you will need to multiply it into the lives of others.

Take some time to flip back over the pages of this book. Write down some key principles you will teach others from each section.

Section 1 – Big Rocks Go First

---

99 David Stark, *Reaching Millennials: Proven Methods for Engaging in a Younger Generation* (Minneapolis, Minnesota: Bethany House Publishers, 2016), 117.

Section 2 – Leading Yourself

Section 3 – Leading Others

Section 4 – Youth Ministry Essentials

Section 5 – Future Focus

A Prayer to Close

My prayer for you is that you would stay close to Jesus and, as you grow with Him, you would lead from that place. I pray you would have faith in a big God who is reconciling all things to Himself. I pray you would experience heaven on earth as God breaks into your life and ministry in surprising ways. I pray you would enjoy God's smile on your life in all you do. I pray you will multiply all that you are graced with to others, in a deeply life-on-life, relational way. May the next generation meet Jesus through the work of your hands and the grace of our God. Bless you my friend, Amen.

APPENDIX 1:

EXAMPLE OF A LEADERS COVENANT

Covenant refers to the act of God freely establishing a mutually binding relationship with human kind. God is a God of relationship and He desires to bless. He uses the act of covenantal relationships as a way to do this. God made covenants with Noah, Abraham, Moses and David and the ultimate covenant was made with Jesus (the new covenant). God's covenants with his people were always to bless them so they will be a blessing to others (see Genesis 12:1-3 – God's covenant with Abraham).

After praying and chatting with our families, as [INSERT MINISTRY NAME HERE] youth leaders we choose to enter into a covenantal relationship between God and [INSERT MINISTRY NAME HERE] and we commit to the following,

- I am committed to loving God and loving others as the primary basis for not only my life and but also my ministry (Matthew 22:37-39).

- I commit to living a lifestyle that is 'above reproach' with my actions honouring God and others, knowing my lifestyle is a model for young people (1 Timothy 3:2-4).

- I commit to being a valuable team member for the full [INSERT YEAR] school year.

- Because I know that teamwork is vital and my presence is important, I commit to attending consistently and being on time.

For [INSERT YEAR], I am making a commitment to the following programs:

- [INSERT MINISTRY NAME HERE] Life Group Leadership

- [INSERT MINISTRY NAME HERE] Worship Leadership

- [INSERT MINISTRY NAME HERE] Community Life Leadership (eg; events, games, etc)

- Schools Outreach Leadership

Name:

Date:

APPENDIX 2:

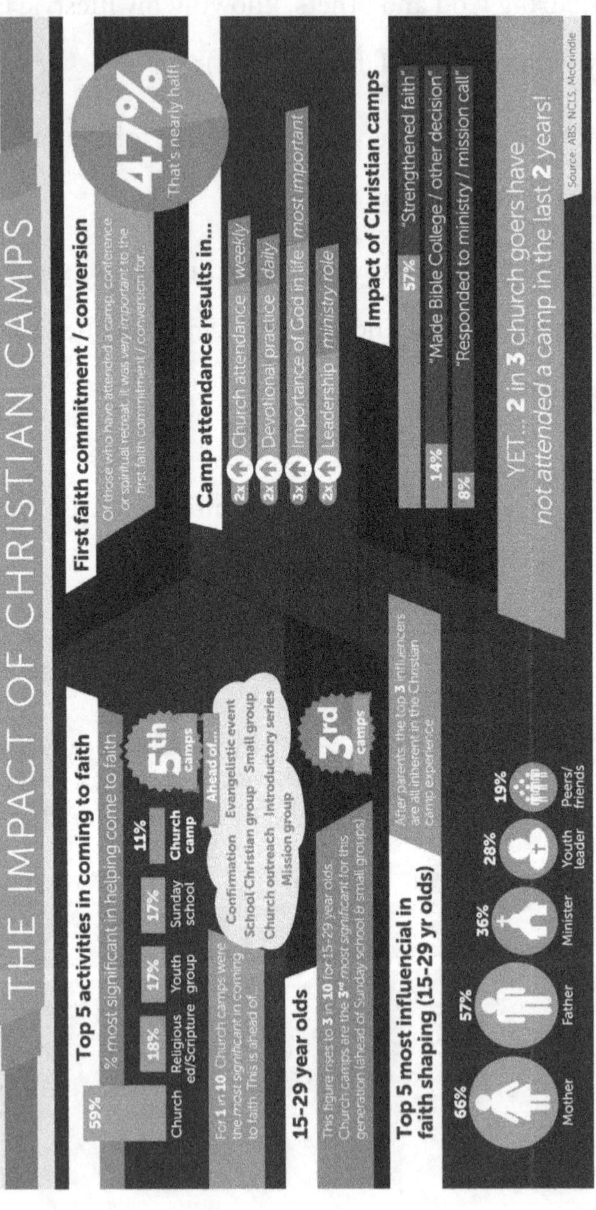

www.christianvenues.org.au/impact/images/CVA_Infographic.pdf accessed 14/04/2017, used with permission

Bibliography

Allen, Holly., and Ross, Christine. Intergenerational Christian Formation: Bringing the Whole Church Together in Ministry, Community and Worship. Downers Grove, Illinois: IVP Academic, 2012.

Barna Group. "Young Adult Study". Ventura, California, 2013. http://www.youngadultlife.com/wp-content/uploads/2015/01/Barna-SDA-Millennials-Report-final.pdf

Barna Group. "5 Reasons Millennials Stay Connected to Church". September 2013, accessed 14/4/2017. https://www.barna.org/barna-update/millennials/635-5-reasons-millennials-stay-connected-to-church#.V6awzuh97IU

Bomar, Chuck. Worlds Apart: Understanding the Mindset and Values of 18-25 year olds. Grand Rapids, Michigan: Zondervan, 2011

Breen, Mike. Building a Discipling Culture: How to Release a Missional Movement by Discipling People like Jesus Did. Pawleys Island, USA: 3dm, 2011.

Breen, Mike. Multiplying Missional Leaders: From Half-Hearted Volunteers to a Mobilised Kingdom Force. Pawleys Island, USA: 3dm, 2012.

Byrne, Dr Ken. Seven Secrets For Hiring The Best People. Victoria, Australia: 2006.

Collins, Jim. Good to Great. London, UK: Random House Business Books, 2001.

Covey, Sean. The 7 Habits of Highly Effective Teens. New York, USA: Fireside, 1998.

Clinton, Robert. The Making of a Leader: Recognising the Lessons and Stages of Leadership Development (2nd Ed). Colorado Springs, USA: NavPress, 2012.

Corney, Peter., and Paddison, Evonne, eds. A Passion For Leadership: Insights From Arrow Australia Leadership Team. Kirrawee, NSW: Arrow Leadership Australia, 2009.

George, Bill. Discover Your True North: Becoming an Authentic Leader, New Jersey, USA: John Wiley & Sons, 2015.

Hybels, Bill. Axiom: Powerful Leadership Proverbs. Grand Rapids, Michigan: Zondervan, 2008.

Joiner, Reggie. Think Orange. Colorado Springs, USA: David Cook Distribution, 2009.

Joiner, Reggie and Nieuwhof, Carey. Parenting Beyond Your Capacity: Connect Your Family to a Wider Community. Colorado Springs, USA: David Cook Distribution, 2010.

Joiner, Reggie, Ivy, Kristen and Campbell, Elle. Creating a Lead Small Culture: Make Your Church a Place Where Kids Belong. Cumming, USA: Orange, 2014.

Kinnaman, David. You Lost Me: Why Young Christians Are Leaving Church and Rethinking Faith. Grand Rapids, Michigan: Baker Books, 2011.

Maxwell, John. C. Developing the Leaders Around You: How to Help Others Reach Their Full Potential. Nashville, Tennessee: Thomas Nelson, 1995.

McCrindle, Mark. The ABC of XYZ: Understanding the Global Generations. Sydney, NSW: UNSW Press, 2011.

McCrindle Research. "Australia in 2020: A Snapshot of the Future". Accessed 14/4/2017. http://mccrindle.com.au/ResearchSummaries/Australia-in-2020-A-Snapshot-of-the-Future.pdf

McCrindle Research. "New Generations at Work: Attracting, Recruiting, Retraining and Training Generation Y". 2006, accessed 14/4/2017.

http://mccrindle.com.au/resources/whitepapers/McCrindle-Research_New-Generations-At-Work-attracting-recruiting-retaining-training-generation-y.pdf

Peterson, Eugene. Eat This Book: The Art of Spiritual Reading. London, UK: Hodder & Stoughton, 2006.

Powell, Dr Kara, Griffin, Brad, and Crawford, Dr Cheryl. Sticky Faith: Youth Worker Ed. Grand Rapids, Michigan: Zondervan, 2011.

Sanders, J. Oswald. Spiritual Leadership (second revision). Chicago: Moody Press, 1994

Shaw, Haydn. Generation IQ: Christianity Isn't Dying, Millennials Aren't the Problem, And the Future is Bright. Carol Stream, Illinois: Tyndale House Publishers, 2015.

Stark, David. Reaching Millennials: Proven Methods for Engaging in a Younger Generation. Minneapolis, Minnesota: Bethany House Publishers, 2016.

Stanely, Andy. Deep and Wide: Creating Churches Unchurched People Love to Attend. Grand Rapids, Michigan: Zondervan, 2012.

Warren, Rick. The Purpose Driven Church: Growth without Compromising Your Message and Mission. Grand Rapids, Michigan: Zondervan, 1995.

Wright, Tom. Paul For Everyone: The Prison Letters. London, UK: SPCK, 2004.

THE GLUE

IF YOU WERE ENCOURAGED AND CHALLENGED BY
ENGAGING WITH THE GLUE, WHY NOT CONSIDER
PURCHASING A COPY FOR EACH OF YOUR YOUTH
TEAM AND STUDYING IT TOGETHER.

GLUE
MIKE STEVENS

PURCHASE COPIES AT
WWW.MIKEBSTEVENS.COM

I so love Mike Stevens. He's not just a friend, he's a great leader. He has lived youth ministry long enough not just to practice it, but to digest what matters most. If you love young people, this book will help you reach more of them sooner all the while helping you figure out how to lead optimally.

Carey Nieuwhof – Author and Founding Pastor, Connexus Church, Canada

Reading the opening section by Mike Stevens was like a breath of fresh air for me. 'Relational discipleship' as the key to effective youth ministry. I'm glad that Mike is taking us back to this core strategy for effective youth ministry. Mike is great practitioner and I commend this book to you.

Bishop Stephen Hale – Lead Minster, St Hilary's Network

Christianity is always one generation from extinction so reaching out and raising up the next generation of Christ-followers is vital. Of course, that is easier said than done, especially in today's rapidly changing culture. That's why I am so thankful for Mike Stevens. I believe that his new book, drawn from years of experience and reflection, will make a significant contribution to helping churches and leaders be more effective in youth ministry. Highly recommended!

Mark Conner – Australian Pastor / Author / Speaker

I got to know Mike when he was serving as a Youth Pastor on our Generational team at Crossway. He is committed to the development of leaders who would walk alongside young people. Mike speaks with clarity, conviction and experience, exploring ways to help young people discover and live out their faith. In this book Mike reminds us of what we know, but can easily miss as we navigate the demands of ministry. A timely reminder that strategic relationships matter.

Rev. Margaret Spicer – Generations Pastor, Crossway Baptist Church

I have had the privilege of knowing Mike for a number of years and seen him not just write great leadership insights but to also put them into practice. This book has been years in the making with leadership tips and wisdom that actually work. This book is a must read for new Youth Pastors but is also brilliant for more seasoned leaders to ensure greater alignment to God's mission.

Kylie Butler – Generations and Emerging Leaders Pastor, Baptist Union of Victoria

Mike Stevens draws from the deep well of many years involved directly in youth ministry in writing *The Glue*. This book is very readable, easy to access and gives plenty of helpful clues in how to build effective youth ministry. Mike does not try to dazzle readers with complex ideas, rather outlines clear and understandable concepts that will challenge youth ministry leaders for the years ahead. The Glue is an essential resource for youth ministry leaders.

Karl Faase – CEO, Olive Tree Media

In an ever increasing individualistic world, Mike offers a personal, practical and passionate plea for leaders to invest in relationships with the next generation. Mike's insights from his own ministry, as well as the leaders he has been surrounded by, provide both gentle challenge and sharp clarity.

Steve Dixon – Associate Director of Youth and Young Adults, Baptist Churches of NSW / ACT

Mike is one of my favourite people to talk ministry and life with over a coffee. This book is like a condensed version of all those conversations. A wealth of inspiration and resource for leaders in all stages of ministry - drawn from years of experience and leaning in to great thinkers and innovators in ministry, market place and life. Grab a coffee and enjoy the chat!
Kimberly Smith – Associate Pastor at Werribee Baptist Church / Speaker / Author

Mike Stevens is the real deal. Mike's patiently invested in me as a leader, mentor, role model and friend. He lives and breathes relational ministry and is relentless in his pursuit of championing this in young people. *The Glue* is a handbook that should go straight into the hands of anyone wanting to passionately sow into the lives of the next generation.
Mike Wardrop – State Youth & Young Adults Coordinator, Uniting Church SA

Having been mentored by him for a number of years, I have seen first hand Mike's heart for young people and the gospel, and experienced the benefit of implementing a relational discipleship approach to youth ministry in my own church context as modelled by Mike's relational investment in me.
Riley Smith – Family Ministries Pastor at Victor Harbor Baptist Church

Mike understands and has led youth ministry like few I've seen. He is one of the best leaders I know. I've greatly appreciated his dedication to helping the young men and women he has led, grow into who they were meant to be as disciples of Jesus. Mike's teaching through this this book is no different. It's genuine. It's practical. It's lived out. Read it. Live it. And watch your youth ministry grow.
Steven Fogg – Blogger and Church Online Expert / Executive Pastor at Derby Church, UK

In *The Glue*, Mike takes his experience of leadership, his passion for discipleship and his value for people and provides us a framework and focus on relational discipleship that is as significant at this point in history & ministry as it has ever been. The call to recalibrate around relationships is a timely challenge and invitation, for not only Youth Leaders but us all.
Rich Robinson – Catalyst and Coach, 3DM Europe

In a decade when we have too few leaders committed to youth ministry Mike stands out as a person with experience, credibility, and a thoughtful approach to leading young people. This book will be helpful to any Christian leader seeking to lead young people well.
Julian Dunham – Arrow Leadership, Developing World

Mike Stevens is a highly relational and genuinely authentic bloke with a heart for effective discipleship and leadership. This book is the result of the coming together of Mike's character, experience and passion. I commend this book to you and believe it will be a blessing to the next generation of leaders – Enjoy!
Rev. Mike Mills – State Executive Minister, BCSA

The Glue, written by someone of the calibre and vast experience of Mike Stevens, is a resource that is essential reading! The principles outlined and the practical know-how contained in this book, has the potential to transform the way we impact young people for Jesus.
Graham Agnew – Leadership Coach and Ministry Team Leader at Blackwood Church of Christ, S.A.